Knit with Style

FERNE GELLER CONE

Madrona Publishers, Inc.   *Seattle*

Connecting Threads

KNIT WITH STYLE
STITCH WITH STYLE
WEAVE WITH STYLE

FOR ALL THOSE WHO CARE

OTHER BOOKS BY FERNE GELLER CONE:

Knit Art, Van Nostrand Reinhold, 1975
Knutty Knitting for Kids, Follett, 1977

Library of Congress Cataloging in Publication Data

Cone, Ferne Geller.
  Knit with style.

  (Connecting threads)
  1. Knitting. I. Title. II. Series.
TT820.C7835   746.4'32   79-13744
ISBN 0-914842-38-2

Acknowledgments

My sincere thanks to Mary Dean Scott, Carol Schimanski, Jane Thompson, Joanne Harris, Gail Sullivan, and Ivarose Bovingdon, who so graciously allowed me to use examples of their work.

To J. Morton Cone, for devoting precious leisure hours to doing the photography; to Barbara Chasan, my editor, who was able to anticipate my thoughts; and to Dan Levant, the publisher, who wholeheartedly embraced the idea of Connecting Threads and *Knit with Style.*

Madrona Publishers, Inc.
2116 Western Avenue
Seattle, Washington 98121

Drawings by Louise Lewis; drawing on pages 11 and 79 by Phil Garland
Knitting needles courtesy of Boye Needle Company

Contents

Style: A distinctive or characteristic manner

Adorning our bodies is one way of exhibiting that precious commodity called individuality—a way of expressing our personality to the world.

Certainly we are aware that clothes and patterns we buy in a store are never individual. Clothes bought off the rack aren't one-of-a-kind, and commercial patterns designed for sewing and knitting are available to everyone. A hand knit can be your personal signature. Apply a few basic techniques. Combine them with an adventurous spirit and your imagination.

A spot of color, a bit of braid, a pocket with a touch of detail, some applied texture, can transform the most mundane knitted sweater or skirt into something uniquely yours.

You can discover how easily hand knitting may be combined with weaving and further enlivened with surface embroidery or any of the other fiber arts, such as crochet, macramé and needle lace. All fiber arts are compatible with each other. If you know any of these crafts, you're already on your way to personalized design and style.

In this book I want to show you how to individualize your knitting—through your choice of yarn, your choice of pattern stitches, the color, and even the size of needles you use—and, most important, how to judge what is flattering garment design for you.

Let me share with you how I learned to design hand knits. Although I learned the basic knitting techniques as a child, I had never cut the umbilical cord. I would knit a prescribed number of inches, trot back to the knit shop and wait

1. Three-piece classic cardigan ensemble. Sweater-jacket knitted of double strands of wool rug yarn in robin's-egg blue and trimmed with ivory. Skirt and sleeveless top of the ivory. Designed and knitted by author.

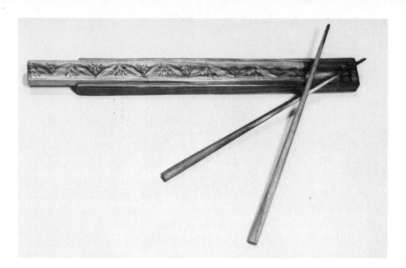

2. *Hand-carved rosewood knitting needles from Bali.*

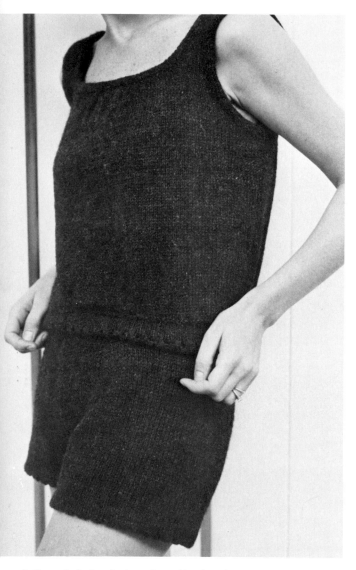

3. *Sunsuit knitted of wool combined with copper metallic yarn. Square neckline with bias binding, picot-stitch hems. Designed and knitted by author. Photo by Larry Rea.*

around for two or three hours until my name was called. The instructor would look at my work and then write (in longhand) the instructions for another few inches. This went on until the garment was completed. Being an impatient soul, I resented having to run downtown for the next batch of instructions. There had to be a better way.

Back in those days, knitted skirts were worked on circular needles, starting from the bottom. Going round and round from the bottom up didn't make much sense to me, and I wondered why a skirt couldn't be knitted in sections from top to bottom, exactly like woven material, and then assembled. Besides, who said it couldn't?

The idea of knitting to a paper pattern intrigued me. I found an easy-sew pattern with good lines and knitted my pieces to conform to the pieces of the paper pattern. Although I'm not much of a dressmaker, I was incorporating simple dressmaking techniques into my knitting methods.

Hand-knitting yarns were limited—only wool, cotton, and linen were available—and even color choices were few; therefore, I concluded that garment design must be my first consideration. Of course, I made some crazy boo-boos and ripped a lot; however, when that first self-designed garment was finally finished, I was delighted because none of my previous hand knits had fit so well. I became intrigued with the many creative possibilities open to me.

2

You could say that I am a classicist. When I spend hours designing and knitting a garment, I want to be sure that the results will be wearable for a very long time. Therefore, I usually stick to basic shapes and rely on texture and color to provide surface drama.

Shape fascinated me, so the main thrust of my very early efforts was in that direction. I could knit any pattern stitch, if I concentrated, but knew I would tire of an abundance of patterned material after only a few wearings. The pattern stitches weren't entirely eliminated. From time to time I would insert a pattern stitch here and there for emphasis or would use a very simple overall pattern for texture.

Good design is as important in hand knitted material as it is in woven material, and a lot easier to redo. How can one decide whether or not a design is good or bad? This is how I do it. Before starting a new project, I decide how and when I want to wear that particular garment. If it suits the type of life I lead and can be worn with other things in my wardrobe, I've made a good choice.

Little details can make a tremendous difference in the finished garment. Do what the designers do—go to the library and look through books of costume and clothing designs. Record details that appeal to you, and try to adapt versions of them to your hand knits.

You'll probably be knitting for other people, too. The recipients will be flattered if your garments reflect your interest in their taste.

How can one keep up with the fashion picture when it changes from season to season? Confidentially, I used to feel exploited by fashion movers and shakers and long ago decided to do my own thing—to wear clothing that made me feel good and that I could forget about while wearing. Then I took a good, long look at myself in the mirror—front, back,

4. "Beaches and Cream" swimsuit cover-up. Knitted of cream and camel linen. All garter stitch. Crocheted trim. Designed and knitted by author.

side, and top to bottom. I suggest you give yourself the same kind of evaluation.

Decide on the colors you feel good in. Nothing can be more frustrating than working with colors that disturb you. It can destroy your enthusiasm and make your efforts a drag. (There have been many studies made which explain how our lives are affected by color.) Knowing my own personality, I stay away from strong, primary colors and stick to the muted tones. Muted colors aren't necessarily drab—they are easier to live with and are more adaptable as basics in my personal wardrobe. Perhaps you feel that way, too. Accessories with a dash of color—a belt or scarf will usually suffice—perk up your outfit.

This book is not intended to give you line-by-line directions for a specific garment. Instead, it suggests ways of using a few simple rules, coupled with awareness and imagination, to produce out-of-the-ordinary, but very wearable, hand knits.

Throughout the years I have been knitting, my enthusiasm for this universal craft has not only been sustained, it has increased. The excitement is still there every time I start a new project. I hope that you will derive some useful, long-term information from these pages and that your enthusiasm will encourage you to experiment on your own and to *Knit with Style!*

Yarns and Yarns

Your well-designed garment will be built from yarn. Before choosing yarn, you should have some knowledge of what's available. For wearables, the most desired yarns are always the naturals—wool, linen, cotton, and silk. In my opinion—and I know others agree—wool is the top of the line. It has a memory; so after many launderings or cleanings it will spring back into shape. Wool also accepts dyes beautifully—the colors are clear and true—and it combines well with other fibers. The Cadillacs of wool are cashmere, Angora, and alpaca.

Linen and cotton, which are plant fibers, have a durability that goes on forever. They are strong, but not elastic. By that I mean they must be knitted to fit. I suggest you add a few extra stitches for a generous seam allowance if you decide to knit with either of these fibers. Linen and cotton are easy to launder and also combine well with other fibers. Against the skin, however, linen feels rather harsh. Cotton is more gentle. These fibers are being used more and more for hand-knit fashions, thanks to the new soft, fluid, unconstructed designs.

Rayon is making a comeback in hand knitting, although now it usually is spun in combination with other yarns, such as cotton or other synthetics, because it has so little body. The high luster of rayon, an early synthetic, is very desirable for special projects, and careful cleaning will help to keep it beautiful for a long time.

5. Samples of hand-knitting yarns.

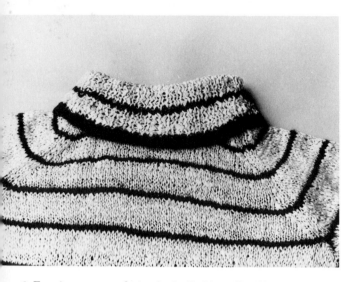

6. Evening sweater knitted of off-white silk ribbon with black wool stripes. Designed and knitted by author.

Silk yarns, when you can still find them, are the Rolls Royces of fibers. They demand very special care, both in the knitting and in the wearing. Often they may split as you knit them.

At one time, knitting with silk ribbon was all the rage, but the garments designed for this material were atrocious, and in those days, it was recommended that the ribbon be kept absolutely flat when knitting. All the dresses I ever saw knitted of this material had a terrible sameness which made them unappealing to me. Don't get me wrong. I didn't dislike the silk ribbon—I just objected to the rigid manner of its use. Again, a little experimentation paid off. I didn't care whether or not the ribbon twisted—in fact, the twisting provided the fabric with more stability.

Silk yarns and ribbon also have little elasticity; so if you decide to work with them, consider carefully the overall design of the garment. It should be designed for maximum movement, because with frequent wear, silk, especially ribbon, will bag and bulge. I can remember many a time, when I had my shop, that a customer would come in distraught because the dress she had knitted from silk ribbon (and for which she spent an enormous amount of money) had sagged so much the garment was almost unfixable. Combining the silk with a fine, matching wool is sometimes a good solution to this problem—at least it will add some elasticity.

Silk ribbon is also difficult to clean, and there are very few cleaners around who know how to handle it. So, unless you know of an exceptionally good and knowledgeable cleaner in your area, try to find another yarn to work with.

Synthetic yarns are flooding the market. I will not describe the many varieties now available for hand knitting, but there are a few important things you should be aware of. Although they offer easy care, usually need no pressing, and can be worn immediately, they must be knitted to fit exactly because their heat sensitivity causes the fibers to wilt, or even to melt in some instances, if steam is applied.

Synthetics do not breathe; therefore, they can be very warm. They also pill excessively and retain stains. Static build-up in synthetics can also be a problem because it attracts dust. So don't be fooled by easy care. Although I do use synthetics occasionally, I really don't enjoy working with them nearly as much as with the naturals. But don't rule out synthetics entirely.

Yarns are interchangeable, too. Should you decide to knit a garment described in a pattern book, but can't find the recommended yarn, don't be discouraged. Substitute something comparable in thickness, texture, and fiber content. Be sure your stitch gauge is the same as that recommended in the pattern. (Most yarn shops have interchangeable yarn charts.)

Acquaint yourself with all the different varieties of yarn now available by spending a little time in your favorite yarn shop. Pinch and squeeze, check to see if samples have been knitted up, and ask lots of questions. Sometimes the samples won't show you all you need to know; so buy a skein or two of yarns that appeal to you and experiment with them. Try some combinations of a flat yarn with a slubbed texture and wool with linen, cotton, or synthetic—then label the samples.

Record your experiments in a notebook. You'll then have a permanent record for future reference. To get a better feel for the material and how it will act, here are some experiments I find useful.

Stretch an all-wool sample out as much as you can vertically and horizontally and pin it to a flat, padded surface. Steam it with your iron on full steam and leave the sample pinned in place until it is thoroughly dry. When you applied the steam did it flatten the yarn? When you remove the pins, does the material creep back to its original size or does it stay put? Do you like the finished appearance? Make notes of your reactions because the information will be invaluable. Do the same experiment with linen and cotton.

Now knit a small sample of a synthetic yarn and steam it as you did the wool. Notice that when the steam comes in contact with the synthetic yarn, the yarn begins to creep. It has no memory—in other words, it will not spring back to its original shape. Now you know why laundering instructions on yarn labels tell you *not* to steam-block synthetics.

7. Steaming a knitted sample.

I have used steam successfully on synthetics, but very cautiously, and only to gain an inch or two in length or width when I've miscalculated. If you want to take a chance, here's how.

Draw an outline of your garment on a large piece of paper. Pin the garment to the paper with your T-pins. Hold the iron a couple of inches above the material and spray steam. With your other hand, flatten the material. Now let it rest, still pinned, until the material is *thoroughly dry*. To add an inch or so in length and width, extend the outline to the desired length and width. Stretch and pin the garment to the extended outline. Now steam and hand-press again. Always be sure the material is completely dry before removing it from the paper outline.

In addition to testing samples by steaming and stretching, I sometimes knit samples and leave them outside to see how they react to the elements. With so much pollution in the air, it's not always possible to predict the results.

Those of you old enough might remember what happened to nylon stockings because of severe air pollution. In some industrial communities, stockings literally disintegrated while they were being worn. Scientists discovered that air pollutants had attacked the nylon fibers. There were many embarrassed women walking around, I can tell you.

Most hand-knitting yarns have laundering instructions, but if you buy your yarn in a shop specializing in weaving supplies, laundering labels are rarely attached. Be sure you ask before you buy, then make samples and launder them.

Once you've experimented and seen for yourself exactly what can happen to yarns under various conditions, you'll be better able to select those suitable to your needs. Not all your experiments will be successful, but you'll certainly come away with some knowledge of what will and what won't work.

Perhaps you think I put too much stress on testing, but my personal experience has proven that one should never take anything for granted. Testing will save you many hours. What good is it to start knitting a garment only to find, after you're well on the way, that the yarn wasn't what you had in mind at all?

Most knitters choose their yarn after they have decided on a design for the garment. Some choose the yarn first. When I particularly like a yarn's color and texture, I'll design my garment to complement them.

The color of your yarn can minimize or dramatize your design. Judicious selection is important. When knitting a garment for yourself, select a color that will flatter your skin tones and your figure and that can be worn with other things in your wardrobe. Remember that strong, primary colors will emphasize areas you might not want to emphasize. Consider also any pattern stitch you might be using. A strong color can be so overpowering as to completely mask the stitch and the design. More neutral colors will allow the design to come forth; then, if you feel the need for more color, add a bright scarf or an interesting piece of jewelry for accent.

8. Triangle shawl knitted from one skein of wool bouclé. Knitted by Mary Dean Scott.

What to Expect
From Your Yarn Shop

As a former yarn shop owner, I would like to share some thoughts with you about what to expect from your yarn shop.

You can expect good service, quality yarns, and advice, but you're the one who will be working with the materials; so it is your responsibility to be candid about the degree of your skills. If you exaggerate them, you'll only get into hot water.

It is the responsibility of the shop owner, in my opinion, to be knowledgeable about the various types of yarn carried in the shop. The shop owner and any employees are usually very gracious about helping to interpret patterns and to suggest alternate yarns, if necessary. There should be a finished garment (or at least a sample) to look at and feel.

It's a real bonus if the owner has some knowledge of clothing design and is able to help you choose a suitable design.

It is important for you to ask specific questions about the shop's return policy before making a purchase. Returns have always been a sticky wicket. If the shop is reliable, it will have a firm policy, and you, the customer, should understand why it is necessary. Of course it's not always possible to anticipate how long it will take to knit a garment, but it's unreasonable to expect the shop to accept a return after the time limit has elapsed. It plays havoc with the inventory, and too many odd balls of yarn can be a tremendous expense to the owner.

When there is doubt that the garment will be finished within the time limit, knit up one skein or ball of yarn and bring it back to be measured vertically and horizontally. From this it is possible to determine closely how much yarn is needed. Purchase an extra skein, especially if the yarn is a glamour variety, in case there might be difficulty in matching dye lots. If alterations or repairs become necessary later on, this extra yarn will be a lifesaver. It's very short-sighted to go into a tailspin about having to keep that extra yarn. How would you feel about spending time and money on a beautiful garment if you ran out of yarn before you finished? Unfortunately, it happens all the time.

Inquire about a layaway policy. Will buying all the yarn for your garment at one time be a drain on your pocketbook? Most shops will allow you to pay for half and put the rest away for a very limited time.

Should you discover a flaw as you are happily knitting away, stop right there and run! don't walk to the yarn shop. Bring your knitting and the remaining yarn with you. A reliable shop will replace the yarn. Restitution can't be made for your time, but at least the yarn will be replaced. The shop can return the whole batch to the manufacturer for replacement, too.

When you knit from a printed pattern, read it over carefully, and if the instructions are not clear, ask someone at the shop to read it for you. Many times I have found printed errors—sometimes mistakes slip through in the proofing, and sometimes there are mathematical errors.

Not only should the yarn shop personnel be knowledgeable about yarns, needles, and other supplies, but I feel it is imperative for them to help you, their customer, to know the limits of your knitting competence. This knowledge will help you avoid undertaking a project beyond your skills, causing frustration and aggravation. After all, knitting should be enjoyable and relaxing as well as productive.

It was a thrill for me to observe my customers' pleasure and confidence as they advanced and began to tackle more complicated techniques successfully, and even more of a thrill came when they created their own designs.

So ask questions—no question is too silly—and become acquainted with the policies of the yarn shop. You'll be doing yourself a favor and the yarn shop will be delighted to have you as a valuable customer.

KNITTING LANGUAGE

Your fingers are itching to get started, I know, but first things first. If you don't know it, learn the knitting language.

The craft of knitting has a special language, much of which is abbreviated. Techniques are repeated frequently and, for the sake of brevity, their descriptions have been reduced to a type of knitter's shorthand. It is important to learn these abbreviations for those times when you choose to knit from a printed pattern.

Certain symbols are also a part of the language, though not all pattern books use the same symbols. Learn the symbols and their variations, and knitting will be more fun.

Stitch (es)	st, sts
Beginning	beg
Knit	k
Purl	p
Increase	inc
Decrease	dec
Contrasting color	cc
Loop(s)	lp(s)
Main color	mc
Slip stitch	sl st
Together	tog
Pattern	pat
Yarn over	yo
Remain(ing)	rem
Repeat	rep
Slip	sl
Pass slip stitch over	psso
Skip	sk
Right hand	rh
Left hand	lh

Knit in back of stitch	kb
Purl in back of stitch	pb
Yarn in front	yf
Yarn in back	yb
Knitwise	kwise
Purlwise	pwise
Double-pointed needle	dpn

Pattern books from England, Canada, and Australia use the words "knitwise" and "purlwise." In the United States we use the expression "slip as if to k (or p)." Both describe the same techniques. The meaning is to slip the stitch as if you were knitting or purling, without actually working it.

Some other expressions you should be aware of include:

Work even: to work without increasing or decreasing.

Double point: double-pointed needle—needle with a point on each end.

Single point: needle with a point on only one end.

Cast or bind off: to lock stitches into place when the piece is completed.

Sometimes there will be a number surrounded by parentheses. If this occurs, work the stitch before the parentheses as many times as the number indicates.

Asterisks are used frequently. When they are, you are to repeat what is described between them.

METRIC MEASUREMENTS

In most countries except the United States, metric measurements are used. The weight of imported yarns is shown in grams. Do yourself a favor and learn the metric table. To help you be prepared, here's a simplified table of the metric measurements you are most likely to use.

1 ounce	= 28.0 grams
1 inch	= 2.5 centimeters (cm)
1 foot	= 30 centimeters or 0.3 meters (m)
39 inches	= 1 meter or 100 centimeters
1 yard	= 90 centimeters

9. Soupçon of pattern. Designed by author.

Pattern Fun and Games

Have you ever gone bananas over a beautiful print dress and then found that, after wearing it a few times, you couldn't stand all that busyness and wondered why you bought it in the first place? Well, too much or a too exotic stitch pattern in a hand knit can have the same effect.

Because I want to wear my hand knits for a long time, I prefer to let the shape of the garment and the texture of the yarn be of prime importance, and then I use a pattern stitch to emphasize, rather than dominate, the total design. Too much pattern can be a distraction; so it should be used cautiously. Use stockinette or garter stitch combined with dressmaker detailing or use a subtle allover fabric stitch. Then focus on good garment design and beautiful yarns to knit with style.

Here are a few of my favorite pattern stitches. They are not overpowering; yet they provide interest and will complement any design, depending on how you use them.

ZIGZAG RIBBING

This stitch works up into a lovely but simple allover pattern. Fig. 10 shows it worked in knitting worsted, and because the pattern has a rather deep texture, a flat yarn is advisable. The pattern is a version of k2, p2 ribbing set over and back to form the zigzag. It has a multiple of 4 stitches so you should cast on any number of stitches that can be divided by 4. To avoid disturbing the pattern when assembling the pieces, add an extra stitch at the beginning and end for a seam allowance.

Rows 1 and 2:	*k2, p2; repeat from *.
Row 3:	k1, *p2, k2; repeat from *, end p2, k1.
Row 4:	p1, *k2, p2; repeat from *, end k2, p1.
Rows 5 and 6:	*p2, k2; repeat from *.
Row 7:	repeat row 4.
Row 8:	repeat row 3.
Rows 9 and 10:	repeat rows 1 and 2.
Row 11:	repeat row 4.
Row 12:	repeat row 3.
Rows 13 and 14:	repeat rows 5 and 6.
Row 15:	repeat row 3.
Row 16:	repeat row 4.

VERTICAL-LADDER STITCH

The vertical-ladder stitch is a combination of the basic stockinette and garter stitches to produce a ladder effect. Bands of the ladder may be inserted anywhere in your garment. In a skirt, insert this stitch down one side or up the middle or, around the neckline of a sweater, as a trim.

This pattern has a multiple of 6 stitches—a stitch on each side of the 4-stitch center panel. The number of stitches in the center panel may be increased, if you wish, or you may want to increase the number of outline stitches on either side of the center panel. Try these variations just for fun.

Row 1:	k1, p4, k1.
Row 2:	p1, k4, p1.
Row 3:	repeat row 1.
Row 4:	repeat row 2.
Row 5:	repeat row 1.
Row 6:	purl.

10. Zigzag rib.

11. Vertical ladder stitch.

12. Fisherman's rib.

13. Double-fabric stitch.

14. Knotted ascot knitted of mohair combining wrapped and garter stitches. Designed by author.

FISHERMAN'S RIB

Used as an allover fabric stitch, this deep rib stitch produces a plush, rich material. Its elasticity makes it very useful for cuffs and sweater bottoms. Start with an even number of stitches. Note that the stitches at the beginning and end of the row serve as seam allowances.

Row 1: k2, *p1, k1 in row below; repeat from * across; end p2.

Row 2: repeat row 1.

DOUBLE-FABRIC STITCH

The double-fabric stitch is very firm; so first try it out on larger needles so you can see the depth. It's very effective for extra-heavy jackets or coats. The pattern has a multiple of 4 stitches.

Row 1: k1, *sl 2 with yf, k2; repeat from *, end sl 2 with yf, k1.

Row 2: k1, p2, *sl 2 with yb, p2; repeat from *, end k1.

WRAPPED STITCH

For a lacy shawl or a summer skirt, the wrapped stitch gets very high marks, and I use it often. It is simply an exaggeration of the stockinette and/or garter stitch: the length of the stitch is determined by the number of wraps. You may start with any number of stitches but be aware that you will be doubling or tripling the number of loops for one row; so be sure to use a needle long enough to accommodate those extra loops. Perhaps this is one time you'd be more comfortable knitting back and forth on a circular needle.

Row 1: *k (or p), wrapping the yarn around the needle twice (or three times)*.

Row 2: *p (or k), letting the extra wraps drop from the needle*.

15. Rebozo knitted of variegated mohair—wrapped and garter stitches combined with single crochet. Designed and knitted by author.

The fabric will gain stability if you add a row or two of garter stitch between the wrapped rows. Don't be scared when the extra loops drop off the needle on the plain rows. You won't lose them.

TWISTED STOCKINETTE STITCH

The easiest fabric stitch of all is made by knitting in the back of every stitch on one row and purling the next. The twisted stitch is firmer than plain stockinette and has just enough surface interest to add a touch of texture. You can use any number of stitches for this one.

Row 1:   kb.
Row 2:   purl.

16. Twisted stockinette stitch.

17. Pretend cable, front view of sweater.

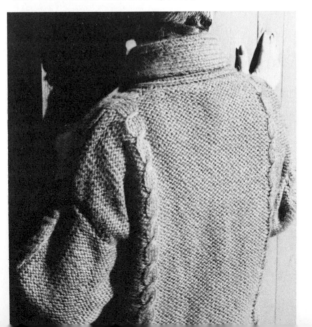

18. Pretend cable, back view of sweater.

CABLES

There are many versions of the popular basic cable stitch commonly used in those lovely Irish fisherman sweaters. Here are three for you to try.

Pretend Cable

The first one I call a pretend cable because it isn't legitimate—the cross-over stitch is a stretched stitch rather than crossing groups of stitches. This is my lazy cable.

Figs. 17 and 18 show how bands of the pretend cable were worked vertically up the sides of the sweater, front and back, and up the middle of each sleeve. The extended cables form bridges or saddles at the shoulders.

Make the cable as many stitches wide as you please, always with an even number of stitches—we'll use a multiple of 8 stitches.

> Row 1: k2, p4, k2.
> Row 2: p2, k4, p2.
> Row 3: repeat row 1.
> Row 4: p2, sk 3 sts, put point of needle knitwise into front of 4th st on left-hand needle

19. Simple cable.

and k, k 3rd st, then 2nd st, then 1st st,
and sl these 4 sts from needle at same
time, p2.
Repeat rows 1 through 4.

Simple Cable

Each panel is made up of 10 stitches.

Row 1: k2, p6, k2.
Row 2: p2, k6, p2.
Row 3: repeat row 1.
Row 4: p2, sl next 3 sts to dpn or cable holder
        and hold in back; k3, k3 from holder, p2.
Repeat rows 1 through 4.

To twist the cable in the opposite direction, put the holder
in front. When you wish to include a vertical row of cable on
each side of the center of your garment, ordinarily one cable
should twist to the right and the other to the left. This gives
balance to the design.

The number of rows between the cable twists may vary, as
may the number of stitches between the cables.

20. Crisscross cable.

Crisscross Cable

This is one of my all-time favorites. It produces a very bulky fabric; so once again try it with larger needles, then with smaller ones. Notice that 8 stitches make up the cable. On one row, the cable is made with the yarn in back; on the other, the cable is made with the yarn in front. The crisscross is achieved by alternating right at the beginning of the row. You may vary the width of the cable by changing the number of stitches in the cable itself, but always use an even number of stitches. Fig. 20 shows this pattern stitch using 6 stitches in the cable; on the row with the cable in front, the pattern is started 3 stitches over from the edge stitches. Knit a single, vertical strip of crisscross cable and applique it to an old sweater for a bit of spice. Use a multiple of 8 sts, plus 4.

Row 1:   k2, purl to last 2 stitches, k2.
Row 2:   knit.
Rows 3 and 4:   repeat rows 1 and 2.
Row 5:   repeat row 1.
Row 6:   k2, *sl next 4 stitches to cable holder or dpn, hold in back, k4, k4 from holder; repeat from *, k2.
Rows 7, 9, 11:   repeat row 1.
Rows 8 and 10:   repeat row 2.
Row 12:   k6, *sl next 4 sts to dpn, hold in front, k4, k4 from dpn; repeat from *, end k6.

Note: If you don't have a cable holder or double-pointed needle, substitute a straightened-out bobby pin.

All of these stitches may be used as allover fabric designs or as inserts to enhance your fabric, and none is very complicated. Try each, just to get the feel of them—work them with different kinds of yarn and sizes of needles. (Remember, a highly textured yarn oftentimes overshadows the pattern, so choose carefully.) Put your samples, with appropriate notes, in your idea notebook.

A fun way to make the most of a pattern stitch is to emphasize some part of your garment by interjecting a soupçon of pattern. For example, in a sweater include a panel of pattern along one side of the front, continue the pattern over the shoulder and down the back. Then carry the pattern stitch to a narrower strip down the center of each sleeve. Knit a skirt to match, and run the pattern panel down the side of the skirt. This vertical pattern continuation is especially flattering to a short or full figure, because the up-and-down pattern sequence gives an illusion of height and slimness. (For a party version, knit the outfit in a metallic yarn or a flat wool combined with the metallic.) See fig. C16.

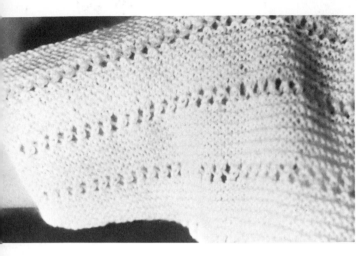

21. *Picot stitches in a no-seam sleeve. Designed by author.*

22. *Basic picot stitch.*

A favorite pattern of mine is a simple openwork picot stitch (yarn over, knit 2 together) that may be adapted many ways. The garments shown in figs. 21, 22, and 23 display several versions of that one pattern stitch. Notice how the stitch has been worked to enhance the overall designs without overshadowing the shapes.

These few pattern stitches are only the tip of the iceberg. Knitting encyclopedias describing hundreds of stitches are available at most needlework shops. But I wanted to introduce you to some of my special favorites; they are not difficult but do provide enough variety of texture to enable you to understand how pattern stitches work. I've given you a design hint or two with each pattern description, but I'm sure you'll become aware of many more possibilities.

23. *Four sweaters knitted with variations of picot stitch. Designed by author.*

Color Changes

Knitting touches of color directly into the fabric is another way to add interest to a simple fabric stitch or garment design. With a stripe or two of a contrasting color, a basic sweater or skirt can be transformed, and it's a perfect way to use leftover yarns. The yarns do not necessarily have to be the same weight or thickness as the main color, but for laundering or cleaning, they should have the same fiber content; for instance, wool should be combined with wool, cotton with cotton, etc.

Do you have a specific color sequence in mind? Then plan, before you start, where you want those specific colors. If you are using up odds and ends, it won't matter.

Stripes may be knitted horizontally or vertically. Remember that horizontal stripes seem to add width and vertical stripes give the illusion of length. Horizontal bands may be worked in any stitch, but try alternating horizontal stripes of garter stitch with stockinette stitch. Vary the number of rows between the stripes. The garter stitch forms a raised texture that produces a nice contrast to the flat stockinette. Match the stripes carefully at the seams when it's time to sew the pieces together.

Vertical stripes demand that you change color within the material itself. This makes them somewhat more time-consuming than horizontal bands, especially when working very narrow stripes. See figs. 26 and C11.

23

24. Uneven stripes of stockinette stitch (right side).

25. Wrong side of stitches in fig. 24.

26. Detail of vertical stripes. See fig. C11.

A tweed pattern can also add an attractive color accent. But a bulky tweed in strong colors will add inches to your figure; so if added inches are of concern, confine such a pattern to trimming necklines or cuffs.

I'm only teasing you with these few color ideas. Since strong color patterns will limit the wearability of a hand knit, use them with restraint. You should know how to handle color changes, however, and I urge you to experiment to determine whether or not you enjoy the challenge.

27. Detail of tweed pattern. See fig. C11.

Gauge—Gauge—Gauge

Gauge is the most important word in the knitting vocabulary. Gauge is the number of stitches and rows to the inch and determines the fit of the garment, whether you work from a commercial pattern or are designing your own garment.

Every knitting pattern is based on a specific gauge which is determined by the type of yarn, the needle size, and the tension used. Unless your own knitting tension corresponds to that gauge with the recommended needle size, you must try a size larger or smaller needle. Even a half stitch, more or less, will add or subtract inches from the width of your garment—and nothing looks chic if it doesn't fit.

When you follow a printed pattern, first you should knit a sample with the needles, yarn, and stitch specified. If the recommended gauge is 5 stitches and 7 rows to the inch on size 8 needles, that's exactly what you should be getting. Are you getting more stitches and rows per inch? Your knitting is too tight, and you should change to a size larger needle. Are you getting less than 5 stitches and 7 rows to the inch? Change to a smaller needle. In other words, use a needle size that will produce the necessary gauge.

Accurately measure your 5-stitches-to-the-inch gauge by casting on a number of stitches that may be divided by five. Work several inches—the larger the sample, the more accurate the gauge. Do not bind off, and always measure the sample on a flat surface, never on your lap. With your ruler, measure off one inch horizontally in the middle of the sample, and place a straight pin at either side of that measurement. If you're on gauge you should have 5 stitches to the inch. If not, now's the time to change needle sizes.

Find the correct row gauge by measuring the sample vertically, although in most instances, correct vertical gauge isn't nearly so important, because it is easier to adjust a vertical measurement than a horizontal measurement.

Knitting tension can vary. When you are uptight your knitting will be, too. When you are relaxed your knitting will be looser. So it's wise to measure your gauge frequently to be sure you are on target.

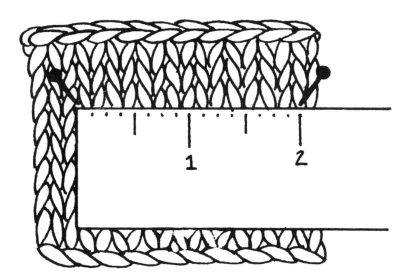

28. *Measuring gauge.*

Knitting to a Paper Pattern

It was a great day for me when I discovered paper-pattern knitting. No longer was I bound by the limitations of printed knitting patterns, and, best of all, everything was laid out for me.

Select a simple commercial paper pattern—one of those easy-to-sew patterns—and be sure it's the correct size. Unfold and lay it out on a flat, padded surface. With your iron at warm, lightly press the pattern pieces to smooth out all the wrinkles and creases.

Let's do the skirt. Measure the width of the front at the waistline (do not include the seam allowance). Then measure the width at the upper hip, the mid-thigh, and finished length. Make a note of these measurements somewhere at the top of the pattern piece.

Multiply the number of stitches per horizontal inch of your stitch gauge by the number of inches at the waistline, and add 2 more stitches for a seam allowance. Working from the top down, increase 1 stitch each side whenever necessary to keep your knitting measures the same as the paper pattern. You'll be able to make any adjustments as you knit. When you reach the desired finished length, knit the hem as described in the section on hems.

Are you planning to incorporate a pattern stitch? Then it's equally important to have a correct gauge for that stitch.

Use a paper pattern for knitting a sweater, too.

Record your results in your notebook—even your mistakes; so you won't make the same ones next time—and keep in mind that you are creating an original hand-knit design that is like no one else's!

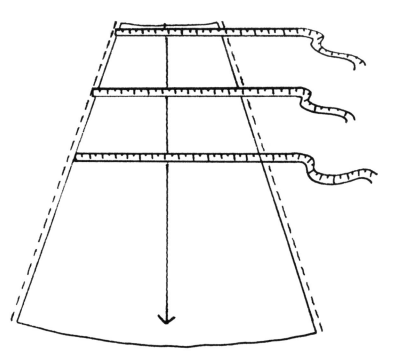

29. *Measuring skirt to a paper pattern.*

C1. (Left) *Man's caftan knitted of rectangles. Ruffled crocheted trim around neckline, down front, and on edges of sleeves. Abstract crocheted medallions on front and back. Designed by author.*

C2. (Right) *Knitted and crocheted rebozo and matching basic sweater with three-quarer sleeve, bateau neckline. Knitted of variegated mohair with matching fringe. Designed and knitted by author.*

C3. *Hooded jacket with shoulder yolk, matching belt, and three-stitch cord at neckline. Designed and knitted by Mary Dean Scott.*

C4. *Squared-off poncho knitted of wool knitting worsted. Garter-stitch squares are joined with single crochet. Knitted by Joanne Harris.*

C5. Seven-eighths tunic knitted of lavendar handspun wool with flecks of cerise. Vertical slash pockets, curved garter-stitch hem, garter-stitch trim down front. Designed and knitted by author.

C6. Mohair V-neck pullover with push-up sleeves and drawstring waist. Crocheted picot-stitch trim. Designed and knitted by author.

C7. Two-piece dress of synthetic bouclé dress yarn. Blouson sweater top, V-neck, push-up sleeves, dropped shoulder. Pattern blocks of picot stitch. Tiered skirt with slashed pockets and crocheted picot-stitch hem. Designed and knitted by author.

C8. Four sweaters showing variations of picot stitch. Designed and knitted by author.

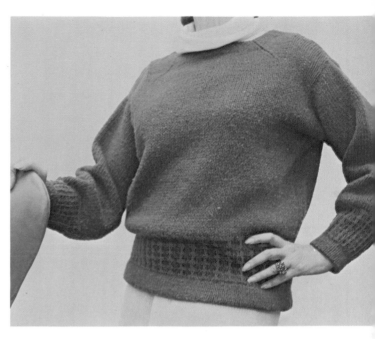

C9. (Left) *Detail of tabbed rolled shirtsleeve.*

C10. (Right) *Ski sweater knitted of rug wool. Border pattern of cerise light-weight wool at hem and sleeves. Designed and knitted by author.*

C11. Pullover skinny vest. Knitted of handspun wool in tweed stitch, chevrons, and vertical stripes. Designed and knitted by Laura Lee Karp.

C12. Shawl knitted of wool with multicolored patterns. Designed and knitted by Gail Sullivan. Photo courtesy of designer.

C13. Halter sweater knitted of recycled Peruvian alpaca yarn. Garter stitch. Matching six-gored skirt—stockinette stitch. Designed and knitted by author.

C14. (Far Left) *Two-piece suit of recycled wool sport yarn in stockinette stitch (see "before" view in fig. 122). Designed and knitted by author.*

C15. *Two-piece evening dress knitted of red and white bouclé dress yarn. Handkerchief six-panel skirt. Matching top with set-in sleeves, square neckline, simple round collar. Designed and knitted by author.*

C16. *Evening ensemble—basic four-gore skirt, matching vest. Knitted of off-white fingering wool yarn combined with gold metallic thread. Gold crocheted trim on vest. Designed and knitted by Ivarose Bovingdon.*

C17. *Three-panel skirt knitted of double strands of wool knitting worsted in garter stitch. Braided belt with tassel. Skirt designed and knitted by author. Belt designed by Sherry De Leon.*

The Parts

Whatever you knit, the attention paid to details will give the garment class and govern the success of your design. The parts make the whole.

It is the details that are important in style and design. Your selection of a hem, the placement of shoulder seams, the shape of a neckline, a pocket, and even a buttonhole—all of these are details to think about when planning a hand-knit garment. The most basic garment may be lifted out of the ordinary simply by the judicious handling of these details.

HEMS

We usually associate hems with skirts. Sleeves, bottoms of sweaters, jackets, coats, and necklines, depending on the design, may also require hems. Let's talk about these hems now, because the hem usually is knitted first.

There is nothing more unsightly than a bulky hem in a hand-knitted garment. Hems should be unobtrusive unless specifically designed otherwise; therefore, for a couturier look, I think it is very important to work them out carefully.

To achieve that professional look, instead of ribbing, add a turned-back hem to the bottom of a sweater and to the sleeves. Do the same with a skirt, providing the yarn you are using isn't too thick and bulky. A bulky yarn will cause the hem to drag and look unsightly.

30. Ski sweater knitted of Swedish rug wool, with border pattern. Knitted mitered neckline, sleeve, and bottom hems. Designed and knitted by author. Photo by Larry Rea.

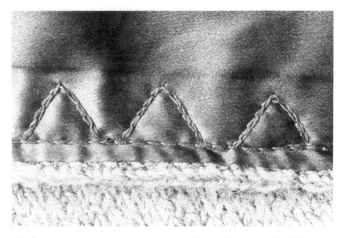

31. Satin lining of coat attached to knitted material with chain-stitch embroidery. Designed and knitted by Carol Schimanski.

29

32. Knitted sweater hem.

33. Knitted hem on recycled skirt.

Horizontal Hem

Let's talk about hemming a sweater. Starting from the bottom, cast on the required number of stitches, but use a size smaller needle than that planned for the body of the sweater. The smaller needle pulls in the material just enough to fit snugly and prevent rippling. Knit about an inch in plain stockinette stitch for the facing; then on the right side, knit 1 row in back of the stitch or purl a row. Knit an inch, change to the next size needle, and continue.

After all the pieces have been knitted and assembled, fold the hem, at the turning row, to the wrong side and pin. Thread your blunt-point tapestry needle with matching yarn and slip-stitch the hem in place by catching each stitch on the cast-on row and barely catching the loop directly above the stitch. It's all right if you happen to split the stitch on the wrong side. More important is that the sewing not show on the right side of the garment. As you sew, stretch the material horizontally after every few stitches in order to keep the hem flexible and the tension even and to prevent popping the stitches when the garment is worn. This also allows for movement during blocking.

Use this same method to hem a skirt, only then you'll be sewing the bound-off instead of the cast-on stitches.

Will you knit a skirt hem? Crochet it? Can't make up your mind? Do what I do. Knit all the pieces and put them on stitch holders until you've decided. Or bind off all the stitches, sew up the seams, pick up stitches along the appropriate edge, and then knit a hem. Are you running out of yarn? Knit the hem with another color yarn as close in weight, texture, and fiber content to the original as possible. It won't show anyway. Or use this other yarn on purpose and add a touch of the new yarn as a trim elsewhere on the garment. Fig. 33 shows how this was accomplished on a many-times recycled outfit.

Crochet a row or two at the bottom of a skirt, and add a picot edge. Figs. 34 and 35 show a triple-tiered skirt made with a bouclé-type yarn. The picot edge is just enough pattern to round out, without obscuring, the skirt design.

Knit an already folded hem directly to the main part of the garment. There's one limitation—you can only work this hem easily on a skirt from the bottom up. But it works well for sweaters and cuffs.

With a size smaller needle, cast on the required number of stitches and knit 1 or 1¼ inches for the facing. Change to larger needles and knit the same number of inches. Fold the facing to the wrong side, leaving the stitches on the left-hand needle. Insert the right-hand needle into the first stitch on the left-hand needle and the first stitch of the cast-on edge and knit both together. Work this way across the row. The hem is automatically knitted into the garment without sewing.

Vertical Hem

Vertical hems, such as facings on sweaters, are made by picking up stitches horizontally after the pieces are assembled rather than by working the facing with the fronts. A vertical hem does help to firm up the edge and keeps its shape well.

Pick up stitches along one front of the garment and knit as wide a band as desired—about 1½ to 2 inches plus the turnback. Bind off loosely. Repeat this on the other front, reversing any necessary shaping. Sew center back seam. Fold in half to wrong side and slip-stitch.

Tubular Hem

Tubular knitting makes an effective and firm hem for cuffs and sweater hemlines. It has lots of elasticity and holds its shape permanently (figs. 38 and 39).

Always with an even number of stitches, loosely cast on the number of stitches required. On the next row increase 1 stitch in *every* stitch. On row 2, knit 1 and slip 1 as if to purl. Work every row this way until the hem is the desired depth. Knit 2 stitches together all across the next row. The hem is completed and you can continue knitting the rest of the section.

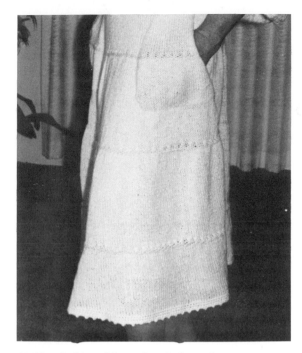

34. *Tiered skirt with crocheted picot edge.*

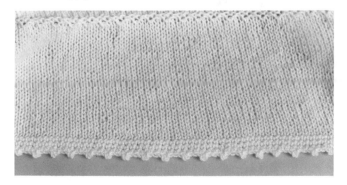

35. *Detail of fig. 34.*

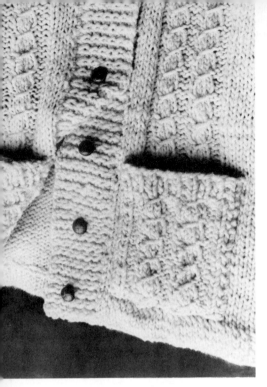

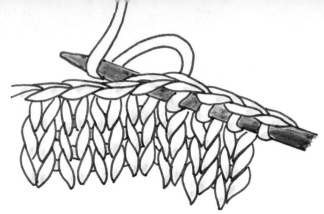

37. *Picking up stitches along edge.*

36. (Left) *Vertical hem as sweater facing.*

38. (Right) *Tubular knit cuff.*

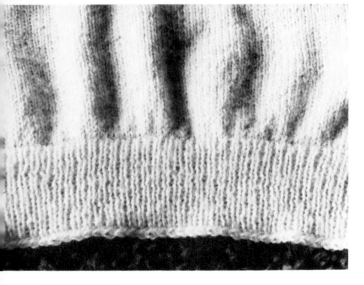

39. *Tubular knit hem.*

40. *Curved hem made by increasing.*

Curved Hem

A curved hem at the bottom of a jacket or coat sweater, or even a skirt, makes an interesting line. There are two ways to achieve this effect—by increasing or by short rows.

Draw the desired curve on graph paper and mark off the number of stitches needed. Each square equals 1 stitch. To shape the curve by increasing, cast on the required stitches less the number for the curve. Then increase 1 stitch at the edge indicated by the graph every row until the curve is achieved. Continue knitting. Assemble your garment; then trim the edge with a bias strip long enough to fit snugly (page 54). You can lay the bias strip directly on the edge of the curve and overcast the strip to the material on each side. Or you can make a rolled bias trim by placing the right side of the material and the right side of the bias together and backstitching the outer edges. Roll the bias trim to the wrong side and slip-stitch the free edge (fig. 84).

Use your graph-paper pattern when shaping a curved edge of a jacket with short rows, too. For a left curve, cast on the required stitches and knit the desired depth, ending on the wrong side. On the next row, work to the last 10 stitches on the left-hand needle and place a marker. Turn your work, slip the first stitch and complete the row. On the next row knit to within the last 9 stitches on the left-hand needle; turn, slip the first stitch, and complete the row. Work this way, adding one stitch at a time from the left side, until all 10 stitches have been worked. End on the wrong side. On the next row knit across all the stitches; then cast on 10 stitches at curved edge for the vertical facing. Reverse this procedure for the right curve. Slip-stitch. The result is very professional.

Angled Hem

An angled hem is useful for vests or a straight-lined jacket.

Cast on the required stitches, less 10, and work 1 row. At the beginning of the next row, increase 1 stitch; complete the row; work 1 row even. Then increase 1 stitch at the be-

41. Curved hem made with short rows (front).

42. Curved hem made with short rows (back).

43. Angled hem (front).

44. Angled hem (back).

ginning of every other row 9 more times. Work 1 row even. Work a turning row, then work the next row even. For the vertical facing, increase 1 stitch at the same edge every other row 10 more times. Your work will look as though you've snipped off the corner. Finish knitting the section. This is the right front. Reverse this procedure for the left front. When you assemble the garment, fold the hem and facing to the wrong side. The edges meet to form a nicely mitered corner. Slip-stitch hem and facing.

Garter-stitch Hem

A garter-stitch hem on a skirt is always reliable because it stays flat and adds a bit of texture, too. After the garment is knitted, work a few rows of garter stitch and bind off. To stabilize the garter-stitch hem and to help the skirt hang properly, before binding off add a stockinette facing.

Proper hemming adds immeasurably to the overall sleek look of your hand knits; so experiment and make notes to yourself about what works and doesn't work for future reference.

SHOULDERS, ARMHOLES, AND SLEEVES

Thank goodness for the relaxed, unconstructed designs in fashion, especially sleeves, armholes, shoulders, and necklines, because they certainly simplify things for knitters. Now that sleeves and armholes no longer need fit so precisely, they are much more comfortable to wear and certainly easier to design.

You experienced knitters probably have followed a pattern for a sweater calling for stair-step bind offs only to find that, when you were all done and had assembled the pieces, the shoulders looked as though you'd inserted football pads and the seams looked simply awful with big holes between the bind offs. Well, knitted fabric molds so beautifully it isn't necessary to bind off in stair steps.

Knit the armhole up to the shoulder. Ignore the stair steps and bind off all the stitches on one row. The material will mold nicely to the shoulder.

My favorite method for finishing a shoulder is to leave all the stitches on the needle of each shoulder, front and back, with right sides facing, and to knit the two shoulders together, binding off at the same time. You'll need three needles to do this. It's not as complicated as it sounds once you get the hang of it. Concentrate on holding the needles parallel to be sure the stitches of each piece are lined up to each other (figs. 45 and 46). You'll love the flat seam, and there's no sewing up.

Raglan

Raglan shaping will always be in style. For one thing, it eliminates the build-up of seams at the shoulder line; when you wear a shirt or blouse underneath, there won't be one seam on top of the other.

First determine the length of the raglan from underarm to collarbone. This time you must gauge the number of rows to the inch, as well as stitches, for the raglan to fit.

An average measurement for the base of the back neckline is about 6 inches across; so if your gauge is 5 stitches to the inch, you should have about 30 stitches remaining after the raglan decreases have been finished.

Work the raglan this way. When you have knit to the underarm of the back, with the right side facing you, *bind off* 2 stitches at the beginning of the next 2 rows. Then *decrease* at the beginning and end of every other row until there are 30 stitches remaining and you've reached the armhole measurement. If you think the decreases are occurring too fast, skip rows between the decreases. If the decreases aren't happening fast enough, decrease every row. Should you end up with a couple of extra stitches, it's O.K. Bury them in the seam when you put the garment together.

Work the front the same as the back, but begin the neckline shaping while continuing the armhole decreases.

Full-fashioned Raglan

To make a full-fashioned raglan, set the decreases 2 stitches in from the edge. With the right side facing you, knit 2 stitches, knit the next 2 together in the back of both

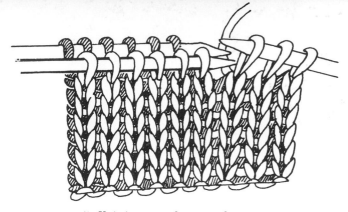

45. Knitting two edges together—step 1.

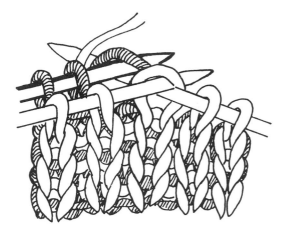

46. Knitting two edges together—step 2.

47. Two shoulders knitted together.

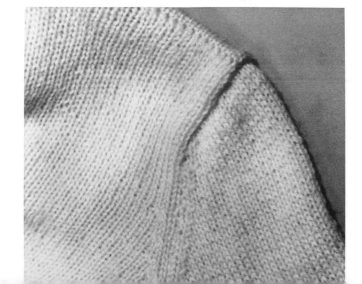

48. Basic raglan.

49. Basic raglan.

50. Full-fashioned raglan.

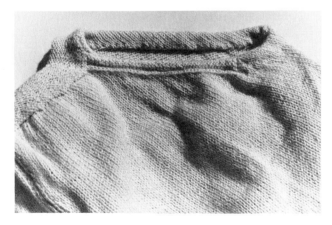

51. Sleeveless raglan with bias facing.

stitches, work across to the last 4 stitches, knit 2 together in the regular manner, knit 2. Notice that the first decrease slants to the left, the second to the right.

Some printed patterns describe this type of decrease like this: k2, sl 1 kl, psso, work across, k2 tog k2. Personally, I think it's easier to just knit the first increase in the back.

Whatever method you use, the average adult measurement for a raglan is about 10 to 11 inches from underarm to collarbone. Determine a child's measurements by measuring the base of the neck from side to side and by measuring from underarm to collarbone. I think children grow too rapidly for there to be an average.

Saddle Shoulder

The saddle shoulder is a combination of raglan and set in and is a favorite because it fits well, it's comfortable, and it's tailored. More than that, it is flattering to narrow shoulders because it gives an illusion of breadth, and it is flattering to broad shoulders because there is no specific shoulder line. The extension of the sleeve forms a bridge over the shoulder line between the front and back sweater pieces. The end of the saddle forms part of the neckline. For the back, measure shoulder width. Decrease as described for raglan until armhole measures about 8 inches, or about 2 inches below the shoulder seam. Bind off. Work the front the same as the back, shaping the neckline, if necessary. Bind off shoulders to match back. To make sleeves, knit up to the armhole. Work armhole same as front and back pieces and bind off stitches at beginning of next 2 rows, leaving a number of stitches equal to 4 inches. Work even on these stitches until piece equals shoulder measurement. Bind off following neck shaping. With right sides together, carefully pin the saddle to the front and back of sweater; then pin armholes, easing in if necessary.

No-shape, Set-in

The easiest armhole of all requires neither underarm shaping nor shoulder shaping—it's knitted straight up. Knit the body of the garment straight up to the shoulders and bind

52. *Saddle shoulder and sleeve.*

53. *Detail of cable used as saddle.*

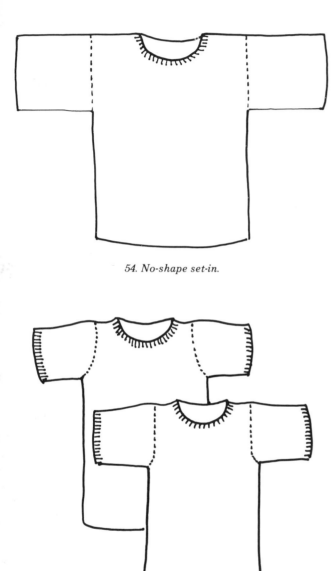

54. No-shape set-in.

55. Shaped set-in with round neckline.

off. Decide the width of the sleeve, cast on the required number of stitches, and knit until you have reached the arm length. Bind off. Sew or knit the shoulder seams of the sweater together; then fold the top edge of the sleeve in half, match this center of the edge to shoulder seam, and with right sides together pin, and then sew, sleeve to sweater. Pin side and sleeve seams and sew one long seam. Turn bottom of sleeve under ½ inch, slip-stitch, and insert elastic, and you have a push-up sleeve. Or knit a ribbed cuff at the beginning, increasing sleeve to desired fullness (figs. 54 and C7).

Raglan Sleeve

Cast on the appropriate number of stitches for your wrist measurement. Work in ribbing for 2 or 3 inches; then increase gradually until the sleeve is the desired width at upper arm. Bind off underarm stitches, and follow shaping to match front and back shoulder armhole shaping. If you have too many stitches, decrease more frequently—if there are too few, decrease less often.

Cuffs

You can knit a cuff separately and sew it to the sleeve later, or you can start with a ribbed cuff. Measure your wrist and cast on the appropriate number of stitches. Use smaller needles than those used for the body of the garment; then change to the larger needles when the cuff is completed.

Make a tubular knit cuff by loosely casting on twice the number of stitches needed for wrist measurement (always an even number) and work, as described on page 31, to desired depth of cuff. Change to larger needles for remainder of sleeve. This firm cuff never loses its shape.

NECKLINES

Round Neckline

It's fun to experiment with different types of necklines, and we'll start with the basic round neck for a classic pullover. About 2½ inches below the shoulder, divide your work in half and measure from the center on either side about 1½ inches. Knit across and bind off the number of stitches that correspond to that measurement. Complete the row. Turn your work and work across to the bound-off stitches; then drop the yarn. Tie on a new ball of yarn at the opposite edge of bound-off stitches and finish the row with this yarn. On the next row knit across the first group of stitches; drop that yarn. Bind off 3 stitches at the beginning of the next group, and complete the row. Turn and work back to the opening; drop the yarn. At the beginning of the second group of stitches, bind off 3 stitches; then complete the row. Bind off stitches as described at the neck edge once more; then decrease 1 stitch each side of neck edge every other row until the desired number of stitches have been decreased. After you have assembled the pieces, pick up stitches around the neck and work in ribbing, garter, or stockinette stitch for about 1½ inches, ending on wrong side. Knit 1 row in back of stitch for a turning row, knit another 1¼ inches, and bind off loosely. Fold to wrong side and slip-stitch. Use a short circular needle or double-pointed needles to work around the neck opening. If the neck-edge stitches are too loose, work 1 row of single crochet around them to even them up before working them on the circular needle or double-pointed needles.

V Neckline

V necklines have been around so long they've become true classics. Vary them by adding a band or two of a contrasting color, by using different ribbings, by outlining the V with a bias strip, or by finishing with a row or two of single crochet.

The average depth of a V is about 9 inches down from the middle of the shoulder. Divide your work in half, and decrease at each neck edge until the desired length is reached and the number of remaining stitches is wide enough for your shoulder.

Pick up an uneven number of stitches around the neckline after the shoulders are sewn or knitted together, and mark the base of the V with a yarn marker. Leave one shoul-

56. Round neckline with facing.

57. Commercial braid strips crocheted together, then stitched to neckline. Designed and knitted by Carol Schimanski.

58. Pullover with ribbed V neckline. Knitted of double strands of weaver's silk and rayon. Patch pockets stitched on horizontally. Designed and knitted by author.

59. Basic V neckline outlined with left and right cables. Designed and knitted by author.

60. Stockinette-stitch V neckline.

61. Horseshoe neckline with ribbed trim.

der unsewn if you intend to use two needles rather than a circular needle. The stitch at the base of the V will serve as the center stitch and is slipped as if to purl. Knit in stockinette or single or double ribbing, decreasing 1 stitch each side of the center slipped stitch on every row until the band is as wide as desired (usually about 1¼ inches). Knit a turning row and a facing as wide as the band, *increasing* each side of slipped stitch. Bind off loosely in pattern, turn facing to wrong side, and slip-stitch.

Square Neckline

Decide where you want to start the square neck. If you intend to wear the sweater over a shirt or another sweater, begin about 10 inches below the shoulder. Determine the number of stitches for each shoulder. Example: 4 inches for each shoulder is average, so with a gauge of 5 stitches to the inch there should be 20 stitches for each side. Work across 20 stitches, bind off the center stitches until there are 19 stitches remaining on the left-hand needle plus the last stitch on the right-hand needle. Finish the row. On the next row work across to the bound-off stitches and drop the yarn. Tie on another ball of yarn and knit the remaining 20 stitches. Work each side with a separate ball of yarn until you've reached the desired length for the neck opening, and bind off. Sew the shoulders together. For the band, with a circular needle a size smaller, pick up stitches around the neckline and place a marker at each of the four corners, making sure you pick up the same number of stitches at each side of the neck. Miter each corner by *decreasing* 1 stitch on each side of each marker, every row. Knit to desired width and work a turning row; then *increase* 1 stitch each side of each marker until the facing is the same width as the right side. Bind off, and slip-stitch facing to wrong side (fig. 30).

Horseshoe Neckline

The horseshoe neckline is a squared neckline with rounded corners. Decide the width of the shoulders by deducting the number of stitches for the base of the horseshoe plus an additional 6 stitches at each side for the base curves. The base of the horseshoe starts with binding off 12 stitches less than the measurement for the square, and then binding off an additional 12 stitches—2 stitches at each neck edge every other row 3 times. Knit even for desired depth, and bind off.

Try all these neck shapings with a flat, wool yarn before you start your garment. These few examples will give you an idea of how neck shapings work. If you have a favorite sweater with an unusual neckline you'd like to reproduce, draw an outline of it on graph paper to help you determine where the shaping should occur.

COLLARS

Sweater collars add distinction to your hand knits. They may be knit separately and sewn on, or stitches may be picked up around the neckline and worked into a collar. My favorite collars include the turtleneck, the cowl, the shawl, and the mandarin—all easy to do.

Turtleneck

The turtleneck has been and always will be popular and is worked from a round neckline base. To make the sewn-on version, measure the number of inches around the neckline. Multiply those by your stitch gauge for the number of cast-on stitches. Work even, in single or double ribbing, until the collar is long enough to roll over one or two times. Bind off loosely in pattern. Use a circular needle to eliminate a seam, or work on straight needles and weave the back seam. Either way is acceptable. Pin the collar to the inside of the neckline and carefully backstitch in place. Remember to keep your sewing and knitting tensions the same.

Or knit the turtleneck by picking up stitches around the neckline. Before doing this, crochet a row around the opening if the stitches seem too loose.

Turtleneck Cowl

I'm particularly fond of this collar because it drapes well and is especially soft and flattering for most people.

The cowl is worked on the same principle as the basic tur-

62. *Horseshoe neckline—machine stitched—on double-breasted jacket.*

63. *Basic turtleneck.*

64. *Mock turtleneck.*

65. Turtleneck cowl.

66. Shawl collar on cardigan.

tleneck; however, instead of knitting even for the entire length of the collar, knit even for about 2½ inches; then decrease evenly across 1 row about every tenth stitch and then every fourth row 3 more times. Knit 4 rows even; then increase evenly every tenth stitch, and repeat the increases every fourth row until the cowl is long enough to fold over and drape. Bind off loosely.

Shawl Collar

Shawl collars on cardigans are practical for warmth and comfortable to wear with almost anything from jeans to dressy clothing. Short rows provide the depth at the back of the neck.

With a 36-inch circular needle a size smaller than that used for the main sweater sections, start at the lower edge of the right front and pick up stitches evenly along that edge, around the neck, and down the left front. Place a marker at the center back. Work even in single rib for 1 inch, ending at lower right front. On next row knit over the marker plus 4 inches. Turn your work, slip the first stitch, and knit over the marker plus 4 inches. Turn, slip the first stitch, and knit across to 3 stitches before the last turn (you will recognize the turn by the space between the stitches); turn again, slip the first stitch, and work to within 3 stitches of the last turn. Work back and forth this way until all the stitches between the first two turns have been worked. These incompleted rows are called "short rows" and they form the neckline depth. After the last turn, complete the row and work back and forth on all the stitches on the needle, inserting buttonholes on the correct side if necessary, until the front bands are as wide as you desire. These form horizontal ribbing. Bind off loosely in pattern.

Set-in Shawl Collar

The set-in shawl collar is a straight piece knitted to fit inside a square neckline. Cast on the same number of stitches as bound off at the base of the square plus two more for seam allowance. Knit even until the collar is as long as the total measurement of the two neck edges plus the back of the neck. Bind off loosely in pattern. Pin the collar to the neck opening, starting with the bound-off edge of the collar and pinning its length along one side of the neck edge, around the neck, and down the other side. Pin the bound-off edge to the base of the square; then pin the cast-on edge on top of that. If the collar seems too short, rip out the bound-off edge and add a few more rows. If it's too long, rip out a few rows. Sew the collar to the neckline. The shawl is formed automatically. The little shawl may also be knitted in garter stitch or a pattern stitch.

Round Collar

Let's assume your sweater has a simple round neckline with a front opening. Measure the circumference of the neckline less about an inch on each side of the front opening. Multiply the number of inches by the number of stitches in your gauge. Cast on that number of stitches. Place a marker between the stitches at each shoulder seam. Knit 2 or 3 rows, ending on the wrong side. Increase 1 stitch each side of the marker every fourth row until the collar is the desired width. Bind off. Turn back the bound-off edge about ½ inch and slip-stitch; see "Putting All the Pieces Together."

For a double sewn-on collar, cast on the correct number of stitches and increase as described. When the collar is the desired width, knit a turning row; then make a facing by decreasing, instead of increasing, the same number of times on each side of the marker. Bind off. Turn the collar wrong side out and backstitch the short sides together as close to the

67. Set-in shawl collar.

68. Round collar.

69. *Mandarin collar.*

70. *Mandarin collar on Connecting Threads coat, part of ensemble combining three crafts. (Story on page 90.)*

edge as possible. Check your tension to be sure the stitches aren't too tight. To attach to the garment, see "Sewing Together."

Mandarin Collar

Make a mandarin collar by picking up stitches evenly spaced around the neck edge of the garment. With a size smaller needle, work even for about 1½ inches, knit a turning row, knit even for 1¼ inches, and bind off. An innerfacing of woven material will help the collar to keep its shape. This should be inserted after the garment has been blocked, so first fold the knitted collar facing to the wrong side and baste. Block the collar; then cut a woven facing to fit the knitted facing and slide it between the folded sections. Now you can slip-stitch the collar to the neckline. (See figs. 69 and 70.)

There are dozens more collar designs to experiment with, and remember, you can copy anything once you get the hang of increasing or decreasing for shape. Don't be afraid to experiment. One of the joys of hand knitting is the freedom to do whatever pleases you. Perhaps you'll invent a collar treatment of your own.

BUTTONHOLES

Learn to make a neat buttonhole and you've added a most important skill to your collection of finishing tricks. A badly done buttonhole can spoil the appearance of your garment. Buttonholes may be horizontal, vertical, or tiny eyelets, and their placement must be decided before starting your project.

First decide where and how large the buttonholes will be. Spacing is usually about 3½ to 4 inches apart on a cardigan sweater, but there are no hard and fast rules. Just be sure that the space between openings doesn't gap.

On a classic cardigan (one that buttons right up to the neck) the first buttonhole should be planned about 1 inch below the neck facing and the last about 1 inch up from the bottom of the sweater. Evenly divide the space between, and mark with colored yarn markers as you knit.

Horizontal Buttonhole

Now's the time to use your row counter for more accurate results. Work both fronts at the same time, knitting in a short strand of yarn in a contrasting color both on the button side and where you intend to make your horizontal buttonhole. Work over to the marked position, knit the next 2 stitches and pull the first stitch over the second (binding off). Work 1 or 2 more bind offs, to fit your button, and finish the row. On the next row, work to within 1 stitch of the bound-off stitches of the previous row. Increase 1 stitch, then cast on 1 stitch less than the bound-off number. This prevents a loose stitch at the corner of the hole. Finish the row. Overcast or buttonhole stitch with matching yarn around the opening for a neat finish. If the yarn is very bulky or a nubby texture, use matching buttonhole twist after the garment is blocked.

Vertical Buttonhole

Position the button for a vertical buttonhole opposite the buttonhole at the halfway mark. The vertical buttonhole should be planned about ⅝ inch in from the edge—3 or 4 stitches, depending on the garment design and the kind of yarn you use. There's no firm rule about this, either. Just be sure the buttonhole is set in far enough from the edge of the garment to prevent strain.

Knit up to the marked space and divide the stitches on each side of the marker. Tie on a second ball of yarn and work both sides at once, knitting up as many rows as

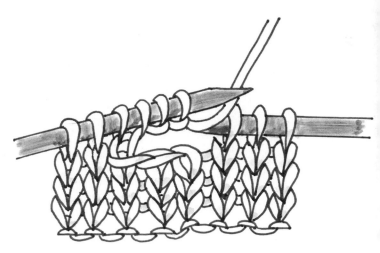

71. *Horizontal buttonhole.*

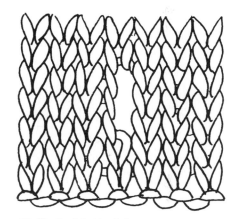

72. *Vertical buttonhole.*

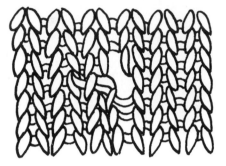

73. Eyelet buttonhole.

necessary to fit the button. (This is the same as knitting two fronts or two sleeves at the same time.) End on the wrong side, drop one strand of yarn, and work across all the stitches. Leave a strand of yarn long enough to stitch around the opening.

Eyelet Buttonhole

This is the easiest buttonhole of all and is particularly appropriate used as a neckline closure or in a series. Knit over to the marker. Yarn over, knit the next 2 stitches together and finish the row. On the next row, work across all the stitches, including the yarn over. Finish the eyelet with overcasting or buttonhole stitch.

Double-Band Buttonholes

If your design has a double knitted band, a buttonhole must be worked in the band and the facing in exactly the same position. For a band 9 stitches wide, plus a 9-stitch facing, on the right side of your sweater (left side facing you), knit 3 stitches, bind off the next 3 stitches, knit 3 more stitches, slip one stitch as if to purl (this forms a turning ridge), repeat the previous steps, purl one stitch, and complete the row. On the next row, cast on stitches over the bound-off stitches of the previous row. This puts the garment buttonhole directly on top of the facing buttonhole. Work a finishing stitch with matching thread or yarn around the garment buttonhole only. Do not stitch the facing buttonhole to the other until after the garment is blocked.

A hint: before you block a garment, baste buttonholes closed so that the openings will not be distorted.

74. Double-breasted blazer knitted in twisted stockinette stitch of bright red knitting worsted with rolled bias trim. Stitched-on patch pockets trimmed with white saddle stitching. Designed and knitted by author.

The Whole

PUTTING ALL THE PIECES TOGETHER

The knitting might be perfect and the pieces all fit together, but the telltale mark of a well-done garment—one you can be proud of—is how carefully each piece is attached to the other.

Sloppy finishing can destroy the whole appearance and even affect the durability of a hand knit. Although the material might be beautiful, if a garment is carelessly put together, if the seams pucker or separate, if the patterns aren't matched, would you be happy wearing it? Therefore, the finishing is at least as important as the actual knitting. Neat assembling and sewing doesn't call for unusual skill—just patience and caution.

Don't expect to be perfect the first time around. I wasn't. After some discouraging results, and many hours of putting together and taking apart, my hand knits finally began to look professional. Skill comes with experience, and take my word for it, it's well worth the effort.

My first seams were always woven because that was the only method I was taught. Eventually, they began to separate, especially at stress points such as underarms and shoulders; and skirt seams were disasters. Finally, frustration forced me to experiment with other ways. I back-stitched those seams with matching yarn, just to see what would happen. When the working yarn was too bulky, I either used a finer yarn, matching the original as closely as possible, or I unplied the bulky and used a single strand. The results were more to my liking, and more important, very sturdy.

I learned to cheat a little, too. By sewing one or two stitches in from the edge, I could hide any loose stitches and could manipulate the pieces by easing them together, if necessary.

You can hide a miscalculation because knitted material is so flexible. If you've misjudged the width of a shoulder seam or the width of the body of a garment (providing the yarn isn't too bulky), it isn't always necessary to rip it out. Make a more generous seam allowance. If you have two or three inches more material than you had anticipated, because your arithmetic was wrong or your stitch gauge didn't work out, you might consider a little gathering along the seam, which, in turn, will give a whole new dimension to your design.

Designers do these kinds of things all the time—turning errors into design. You can, too.

There are many ways to assemble hand knits—backstitching, crocheting, weaving, and even, in some instances, overcasting and machine sewing.

When you are planning your garment, add a stitch or two for a selvedge or seam allowance. This works especially well when your knitted fabric has an allover pattern stitch. Patterns should meet perfectly at the seams, and that extra stitch or two allows for some breathing space. It also prevents disturbing the pattern sequence.

No matter what method you use, use plenty of T-pins to match up the pieces and to control any curled edges. Then baste all the edges together so you can try on the garment before the final stitching.

SEWING TOGETHER

To assemble and sew a sweater, with the right sides facing, pin the front and back shoulder seams together, easing in, if necessary. Backstitch each shoulder seam. Pin the shoulder edge of one sleeve to the front and back. Backstitch. After sewing the sleeve in place, still with the right

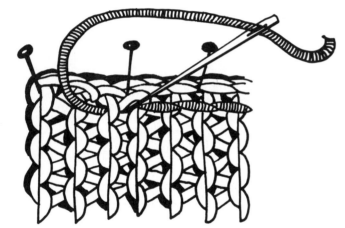

75. Backstitching seam.

sides together, pin the underarm edges together from cuff to armhole and all the way down the side of the sweater, carefully matching underarm seams; then backstitch, again easing in, if necessary. This makes one long, continuous seam (fig. 75). To fasten securely, work two or three stitches over the last back stitch, cut the yarn, and weave the end back into the seam. Lightly flatten the seam on the wrong side—don't press.

Save the collar (if there is one) for last. First pin the collar to the neckline, and ease in, if necessary. Be sure the right side of the collar is outside. Then carefully backstitch, keeping the same tension as your knitting.

To attach a double collar, with the right side of the collar facing the right side of the garment, pin the underside (or facing) to the neckline and backstitch. Lay the topside of the collar over the seam, pin in place, easing in, if necessary, and slip-stitch. Because this is another stress point, be sure the backstitching is the same tension as your knitting to avoid popping the stitches.

If your sweater has a hem instead of ribbing, slip-stitch the hem after all the other seams have been sewn.

Many sweaters have a front band to accommodate buttons and buttonholes. This band gets a lot of wear, so use backstitch here, too, rather than weaving, because eventually the weaving will begin to separate. Again, if you use bulky or thick-and-thin yarn, try to find a matching sport weight for a neater seam.

Whatever you use to sew up your knitted garments, just be sure the fiber content is compatible with the fiber content of the yarn used in the knitted material—wool with wool, synthetic with synthetic—or you'll create laundering or cleaning problems.

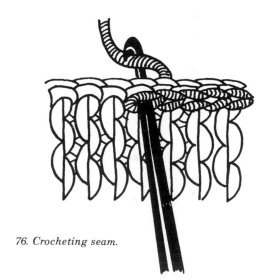

76. *Crocheting seam.*

CROCHETING SEAMS

Crocheting a seam might be the answer in some instances. A crocheted seam is bulkier than the backstitched seam, and great care must be taken to be sure the edge stitches are neatly tucked in. You can't cheat as much with this seam, but crocheting is easier to remove if alterations are necessary or if you decide to recycle.

A crocheted slip stitch is neater and flatter than single crochet. However, you must constantly be on the alert to keep the slip stitch the same tension as your knitting. Here's how.

With right sides together, pin as usual. Put the crochet hook through the two edges, catching both sides of the edge stitches, and pull up a loop. Leave that loop on the hook and put the hook through the next edge stitches. Pull up another loop and pull that one through the loop already on the hook. Continue this way along the entire length of the seam. Cut the yarn, leaving a 3-inch tail, and pull the tail through the loop on the crochet hook.

For a single-crocheted seam, put the hook through both edges and pull up a loop. Leave the loop on the hook and put the crochet hook through the next edge stitches and work a single crochet. This leaves a definite ridge, which is why it's somewhat bulkier than the slip stitch.

Try both ways and judge for yourself. Keep a record of your results.

A crocheted join on the right side of a garment can be decorative as well as utilitarian (figs. 76 and C4). When joining seams so the crocheted edge is intentionally visible, use either matching or contrasting yarn. Neatly done, the crocheted join will add a touch of pizzazz.

For practical reasons, I prefer a crocheted join for children's garments. They outgrow their clothes so fast, and the crocheted seam is a simple matter to unravel, as I said earlier. Just unlock the last stitch and pull that thread. With one movement you can remove the join and then go about the business of making the necessary alteration. It's certainly a timesaver.

WEAVING SEAMS

Ordinarily, I avoid weaving seams, if possible. However, sometimes there are no-stress areas where weaving works better than other joining methods because the connection is flat and almost invisible; for example, the underside of a turtleneck, or a turned-back cuff which should be connected on the right side. So even though you may not use this method often, you should add the skill to your knitting know-how.

Thread your tapestry needle with matching yarn. Lay out the sections to be connected, right sides facing you, edges butted together, and place your T-pins crosswise across the seam, matching one side to the other. Start at the lower right edge and insert the needle through the first stitch; then catch the corresponding stitch on the left side from bottom to top. Work back and forth this way, adjusting the sides as you work to be sure they are aligned. If there is a pattern stitch, be sure the patterns match at the seam edge, and remember your tension.

SEWING-MACHINE JOINS

My second most favorite way to sew hand-knit material is to use the sewing machine. Despite some criticism of this technique, I like the appearance. Bulky or textured yarns may get caught up in the sewing needle, so I use this technique only with lightweight or medium-weight flat yarns.

First pin and baste. Then, with your machine set at the longest stitch, sew together the shoulders, the sleeves, and, finally, the underarms and sides.

Add collars, pockets, and any other trims after you've assembled everything else.

Remove the basting stitches and lightly steam the seams on the wrong side. Turn the garment right side out and lightly steam the seams again. Don't press.

OVERCASTING

When stress is not a consideration and I intend the seam to be decorative, I'll resort to overcasting. Even then, I usually will backstitch on the wrong side first, then overcast. To emphasize a join, overcast with contrasting yarn and make the join an integral part of the original design.

77. *Weaving seam.*

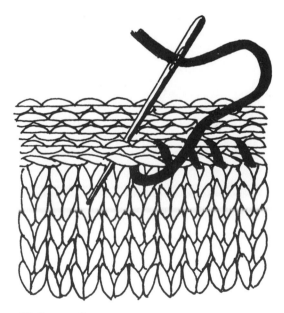

78. *Overcasting seam.*

79. Seam binding cross-stitched to shoulder seam.

80. Two-piece dress with welting on bodice and sleeves. Knitted of maroon wool. Self-covered button trim and belt. Designed and knitted by author. Photo by Larry Rea.

LACING

Try lacing a sweater together if the yarn seems too bulky for a more conventional closure. Select a cord or suede lacing that will fit easily through the knitted material. Work the lacing back and forth; then knot the ends so it won't work loose.

FINISHING TIPS

To prevent a shoulder seam from sagging, stabilize it with a length of seam binding tacked to the seam, straddling the joined area. This should be done after the garment has been blocked. Here's how. Cut a length of seam binding about one inch longer than the shoulder seam and pin it in place, tucking the raw ends underneath. With matching thread, work a cross stitch along the length of the binding.

If the waistline seam in your one-piece dress won't stay where it belongs, tack seam binding to that seam, too, but only if there is a side, back, or front opening, or else you won't be able to slip into the dress. When there is no opening, use narrow, lightweight elastic and stitch it to the seam on the wrong side.

A welting across the back of a sweater or jacket is one of the smartest ways I know to add a couturier touch to a hand knit. The welting may be worked either in stockinette or garter stitch and may be positioned anywhere between the base of the armhole and the shoulder seam. Personally, I prefer a welting about halfway between. In any case, you should knit the back at least one inch longer than the front to accomodate this detail (figs. 80 and 81).

Knit the back up to about the middle of the armhole, ending on the right side. Carrying a strand of contrasting yarn along with your main yarn, work the next row on the wrong side to define the base of the welt. Knit even with only the main yarn for another inch, ending on the wrong side. Fold the material at the marked row to the wrong side. Insert the point of the right-hand needle into the back of the first loop on the left-hand needle, and pick up the loop from the material immediately in back of the loop on the needle. Knit the 2 loops together. Work this way all along the row. The welting is formed on the right side. Remove the contrasting yarn and finish the armhole as planned.

Insert a welt across the shoulder of a blouson by decreasing every other stitch on the right side just before you start the welt. You'll have a gathered effect immediately beneath the welt. This takes care of extra fullness and gives a smooth shoulder line at the same time. Try a sample first.

TRICKS AND TRIMS

Surface adornments and how you use them will certainly contribute to your knitting style. After your garment has been assembled and all the loose ends woven in, think about the trimmings.

Leather or suede patches or binding give an elegant look to an otherwise plain garment. Metallic threads may be woven through the fabric for a dressier look.

A simple caftan knitted in rectangles becomes wearable art by the addition of crocheted ruffles down the front and

81. Detail of welting.

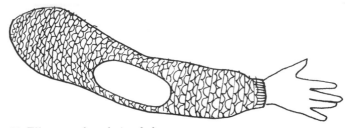

82. Elbow patch on knitted sleeve.

83. Crocheted trim on simple slashed neckline—hand-carved buttons. Designed and knitted by Jane Thompson.

84. Rolled bias binding. Designed by author.

around the neckline and sleeves. Oversized multicolored medallions were crocheted and appliquéd to the back and to one side of the front for surface interest (fig. C1).

Would a fringe at the bottom of a sweater or skirt add a bit of class? Completely cover sweater sleeves with matching fringe. Tassels and fringe smarten up any hand knit. They are easy to make and attach and are replaced easily when you tire of them. Use these or bias trim to finish a decorative belt or to provide a touch of texture or color to an otherwise simple garment. Add interesting buttons to a shoulder or to pocket facings. How about an eye-catching pocket for decoration? Surface embroidery or crochet can add a unique touch to a hand knit. Other ideas will occur to you as you work along.

Bias Binding

A bias binding can take the place of ribbing or a hem. The binding may be made in any width and is most effective knitted in stockinette or garter stitch. It also can be knitted slanting either to the right or to the left. Cast on any number of stitches. For row 1 of right bias, increase 1 stitch in first stitch, work across and knit the last 2 stitches together. Knit or purl row 2. For row 1 of left bias, knit 2 stitches together, work across, and increase 1 stitch in last stitch. Knit or purl row 2. Repeat these 2 rows until your bias strip is as long as necessary and bind off (fig. 84).

Pockets

Almost every hand knit I own has a pocket somewhere. I like to use them for surface interest and because I want a

85. Crocheted trim on knitted patch pocket. Courtesy of Carol Schimanski.

86. Scooped stitched-on pocket.

place to put my hands. There are two basic techniques—stitched on or knitted in. In either situation, try to plan ahead.

Stitched-on Pockets. Pockets stitched on the fabric are easiest because they are usually added after the garment is all finished. Add a pocket anywhere, but be sure it is in scale with the rest of the garment. If your knitting includes a pattern stitch, incorporate the stitch in the pocket, and line it up with the fabric pattern.

Knit a pocket from the same yarn and bind it with a contrasting color; then sew it on anywhere you please. Before sewing the pocket to the garment, lightly steam it; then cut a piece of lining material to fit, and tack it to the wrong side. Turn under the raw edges of the lining and slip-stitch to the knitted pocket with matching thread. Pin the pocket to the material and overcast with tiny stitches of matching yarn around the three sides. Avoid pulling the overcast stitches too tightly.

Horizontal inserted pocket. Before knitting the front of your jacket or sweater, decide on the size and placement of the inserted pocket or pockets. You make the inside flap first. Cast on and knit the desired number of stitches and inches, ending on the wrong side, and place them on a holder. Knit the main segment of the garment, working until you reach the desired depth, including the vertical length of the pocket. End with the right side of the material facing you. Knit across to the space previously allocated for the pocket opening, bind off the number of stitches equal to those on the holder, and complete the row. On the next row, work back to the bound-off stitches, knit the stitches from the holder, and complete the row. There might be

55

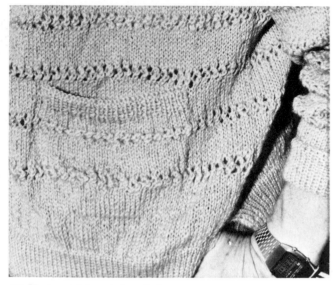

87. Horizontal inserted pocket.

88. Double horizontal inserted pockets with contrasting trim.

a loose stitch where the pocket flap joins the main fabric. Don't worry about it—you can weave it in when you slip-stitch the flap to the main fabric. Pick up stitches along the bound-off row of the pocket opening, and knit another inch or so for a facing. Turn the facing to the inside and slip-stitch. This is a horizontal pocket. Turn the sweater to the wrong side and pin and then sew the three sides of the pocket flap.

Vertical Slash Pocket. Now we'll do a vertical slash pocket. We'll start with a right-opening pocket. Knit the main segment until you reach the desired position for the bottom of the pocket opening. With the right side facing you, knit across to the pocket-opening position and slide the remaining stitches onto a holder. Cast 5 stitches (these are the facing stitches) onto the right-hand needle and work back and forth on all the stitches on this needle until you have worked the desired depth of the pocket—end on the right side. At the beginning of the next row, bind off the 5 facing stitches and finish the row. Cut the yarn. Place these stitches on a holder.

Now we'll work the remaining stitches. Put these stitches back on the left-hand needle, with right side of the work facing you. Cast the required stitches for the pocket flap onto the left-hand needle at the beginning of the row and knit across all the stitches on the needle. Work back and forth until that piece is the same depth as the other side. End on the wrong side. On the next row, bind off the cast-on flap stitches and finish the row. Turn, and work across the remaining stitches plus the stitches from the holder. You have connected the two sides of the vertical opening at the top of the pocket. Finish knitting that section. To complete

56

the pocket, fold the pocket facing to the wrong side and slip-stitch. Turn section to wrong side; pin, then sew the three free flap edges to the body of the garment. Reverse the whole procedure for a left-opening slash pocket.

Kangaroo Insert Pockets. Kids and adults alike enjoy kangaroo pockets. They're handy for carrying small objects and for keeping your hands warm when it's cold. These pockets are usually found on sweat shirts, but fashion designers have discovered their practical use for other garments as well. The kangaroo pocket is simply a vertical pocket open at each side.

Knit the bottom of the sweater, plus another six or seven inches. Leave these stitches on the needle. Turn your work upside down; the bottom of the sweater is on top. Where the ribbing or hem joins the body of the garment, with a third needle, right side toward you, pick up the number of stitches appropriate for the width of the pocket. For instance, if you are working on 80 stitches, figure about 36 stitches for the pouch centered between the two side edges, and leave 22 stitches for each side. On the next row work the first 4 or 5 stitches in garter stitch for the pocket trim, work across to the last 4 or 5 stitches, and work these in garter stitch. Work even, knitting the first and last stitches as described, until piece measures the same as material on the other needle; end on the right side. With the third needle, knit 22 stitches from the needle holding the sweater; then, holding the pocket and sweater needles parallel to each other, put the point of the right-hand needle into the back loop of the first stitch from the front needle and into the front loop of the first stitch from the back needle. Knit these together. Knit the rest of the stitches from the front needle with the corres-

57

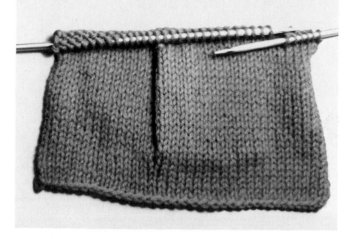

89. *Vertical slash pocket (right side).*

90. *Vertical slash pocket (wrong side).*

91. *Kangaroo pocket.*

ponding stitches from the back needle in this manner. You have joined the pocket to the body of the sweater. (This principle is the same as that used to knit shoulder seams together.)

For a change, you could knit the kangaroo pocket in a contrasting color, then use a touch of that color around the cuffs or to outline the neckline.

Highlight a seam or pocket with a band of suede or leather. This should be done after blocking. Be sure the leather or suede is soft and pliable and not too heavy. Cut ½-inch strips and stitch them to the knitted fabric with your sewing machine. Be sure to use a ball-point sewing-machine needle for this procedure. A regular needle will slice the leather or suede.

Skirts

"I can't wear a knit skirt; my bottom is too big." "Knit skirts make me look fat." "Knitting round and round on all those stitches will drive me crazy." These are only a few of the derogatory remarks I've heard about hand-knit skirts, and they're really not true, you know.

A well-designed hand-knit skirt is appropriate for any figure. I can already hear moans and groans from those of you whose figures are more generously endowed or whose figures may be less than perfect. But when the design is right and the proper yarn is chosen, a hand-knit skirt is as wearable and flattering as a woven skirt, and even more practical, because it can be easily switched from back to front, and also from side to side.

No one has a perfect figure. One hip can be two or more inches higher than the other; some waistlines are high and some are low. If you sew, you know that these figure adjustments must be worked out before the material is cut. This isn't always necessary with hand-knitted material, because it will mold to the body and may be adjusted as you knit. This allows you a measure of freedom—if you goof, just rip out a few rows to correct the sizing. Whether yours is a tiny, petite figure or a more generous one, be grateful for the flexibility of your hand-knitted material.

In years past, hand-knitted skirts were always designed to be worked on circular needles, starting from the bottom and working up to the waistline. I'll never understand why.

Keeping all those hundreds of stitches from twisting on the needle is so frustrating, going round and round so boring, and, somehow, the results always have that "loving hands at home" look.

I've always found it more practical to start from the top and work down, adding width and making other adjustments along the way, if necessary. I knit the panels and then construct my skirts with proper seaming.

The hem is always one of the very last steps in the construction of woven material, so why not plan a hand-knit skirt the same way? Fashions change and so do our figures. Skirt lengths are always changing. One season they're long, the next they're short. When knitting from top to bottom, it's a lot easier to alter those precious hand knits we've spent so many hours manufacturing.

Take your time selecting the yarn for your skirt. If this is your first hand-knitted skirt, use a flat, wool yarn, because the stitches are easy to see and wool is flexible. For the more generous figure, keep to the lightweight, or medium-weight, flat yarns. These will add the least amount of bulk. The heavier yarns or thick-and-thins add unwanted inches, and who needs that? If you must have a bit of texture, try a dress-weight wool bouclé. The texture is slight and evenly distributed and, thus, less overwhelming. When in doubt, your yarn-shop operator should be able to help you make a suitable selection.

This section will explain how to plan several kinds of hand-knitted skirts, suitable for any figure, using a basic set of guidelines.

After selecting your yarn, take your measurements—loose body measurements. In other words, wrap the tape measure around you with two fingers holding the tape in place between your body and the tape measure. Start with your waist measurement. Then place the tape measure at your upper hipbone and take that measurement. Next, measure at the heaviest part of your thigh. After the thigh measurement, add stitches to determine the width at the bottom of the skirt. If you have a favorite skirt, use its bottom measurement as a guide. To help you visualize these steps, make a simple drawing and mark the measured areas.

After you have determined the number of stitches needed at the waist, upper hip, heaviest part of the thigh, and bottom, decide the approximate length, remembering that you don't have to be specific.

Now it's time to knit some swatches to determine the stitch gauge. Cast on 25 or 30 stitches. Try several sizes of needles and knit a couple of inches on each size, placing a dividing marker between each sample. Make a note of the gauge and needle size each time you change needles. Do this for every garment you ever make.

Look at each sample. Which appeals to you most? Remember, the smaller the needle, the firmer the weave, and vice versa. You're the designer; the decision is yours.

A-LINE SKIRT

For those of us with less than perfect figures, the A-line skirt is the most wearable, and so I'll discuss it first.

Multiply the number of stitches to the inch horizontally by the number of inches at the waistline. For example, if your loose waist measurement is 28 inches and your gauge is 6 stitches to the inch, multiply 28 by 6—168 stitches. This is the number of stitches for both front and back. Divide 168 in half—84 stitches, add 2 stitches for a small seam allowance, and you have the number of stitches needed to cast on for the top of the skirt front: in this case, 86. Knit even for 1½ inches. This is casing for the elastic.

The general rule is that the hip measurement will be approximately 10 inches larger around than the waist—5 inches for the front. You'll, therefore, need to increase 1 stitch at each side, evenly spaced from waist to hipline, 15 times or 30 stitches. You will then have 116 stitches. Continue increasing 1 stitch each side about every 2½ inches until you have reached the desired length. This rate of increase will give you a very gradual A-line.

When you've reached the desired length, on the right side, knit one row in the back of each stitch for a turning row, change to one size smaller needles, knit another 1 or 1½

Back   Front

92. A-line skirt.

inches for the hem, and bind off loosely. Some people like to purl 1 row on the right side for a turning row, but I, personally, prefer the knit in the back of the stitch method—it's much neater and less noticeable.

Because correct seaming will help your hand-knit skirt hang better, the basic A-line should have two side seams and a center back seam. The strength and weight of the center back seam hold the material away from the body and will eliminate that ugly seat bulge (or sausage-casing look) which frequently occurs with a two-seam skirt or one knit with circular needles.

The sum of the stitches of the two back panels should equal that of the single front panel. Include a couple of extra stitches on each panel for seam allowance. If your bottom is a bit rounder than your front, blocking will adjust the skirt to the shape. Notice that on the single front panel, increasing is done on both sides; whereas on the two back panels, increasing is done on the side edges, and the center seam remains straight. If you decide to insert a zipper closing, that back seam provides a natural opening.

For the back, divide 84 in half—42—and add 2 stitches to each panel for the seam allowance. Working both panels at once, using 2 balls of yarn, cast on 44 stitches for each back panel, and increase at the same rate for each side as you did for the front. *Do not increase at the center seam.* At desired length, work a turning row, change to one size smaller needles, knit another 1 or 1½ inches, and bind off loosely. Sew the three panels together; then loosely slip-stitch the hem.

GORED SKIRT

Also flattering to most figures is the gored skirt. With the addition or subtraction of gores, it is easily adjusted to fit.

We'll start with a four-gored skirt, so that the skirt may be turned from side to side or back to front. Additional gores should be planned in multiples of 2. In other words,

Front   *Back*

93. Four-gore skirt.

Front   *Back*

94. *Gored/flared skirt.*

95. *Flared skirt—knitted of sport-weight wool yarn. Self-hemmed.*

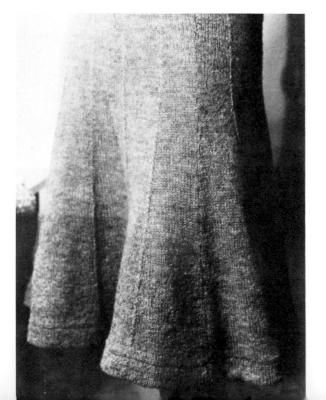

there really is no back or front (unless you decide to insert a zipper). There are decided advantages to a hand-knitted gored skirt; not only is the bulge eliminated, but by switching it around, the wear and tear is evenly distributed. For appearances sake, be sure the gores sit evenly on your body.

Plan the four-gored skirt by dividing the number of stitches by 4; then add 2 stitches to each section for the seam allowance. Essentially, the gored skirt is a variation of the basic A-line, except the front panel is divided into two sections to match the two back panels and increases are added at each side of each of the panels.

Knit two panels at the same time (using separate balls of yarn) to be sure the gauge and measurements are the same and that shapings occur on the same row. At desired length, knit a turning row, change to size smaller needles, and knit the hem. Bind off loosely. Sew pieces together, turn hem to wrong side, and slip-stitch loosely.

FLARED SKIRT

The flared skirt, my favorite skirt, is an exaggeration of the basic gored skirt. The flare is achieved by escalating the number of increases, beginning at a point about 4 inches above the knee. The flared skirt has held its own, fashion-wise, for a very long time and is extremely flattering to hip-heavy figures because the extra width at the bottom balances the hipline, giving a more fluid look.

For best results, with this style use a sport or lighter-weight yarn.

We'll start with six panels. Divide the number of waistline stitches by 6 and add 2. This will give you the number of stitches, including seam allowance, to start each panel. Knit two or three panels at the same time on one pair of needles. Increase as described for the gored skirt, but at about 4 inches above the knee, double the rate of increasing until you've reached the desired length and width. If you have been increasing every 1½ inches, begin increasing every ¾ inch. Work a turning row, change to a size smaller needles, and knit the hem. Bind off loosely. Make six panels. Back-stitch panels together with matching yarn. Turn up hem and slip-stitch in place. Not too tightly!

TWO-SEAM GORED/FLARED SKIRT

A gored and flared effect is possible with only two seams by dividing the front and back into four or six sections, depending on your personal preference. Instead of knitting separate panels, define the gores with a slip stitch. Increases occur at each side of the slip stitch at regular intervals, beginning about 1½ inches below the bottom of the waistline casing and continuing to the hem. Place a marker before each slip stitch to remind you where to increase. When it's time for the hem, knit a turning row and knit the hem plain to avoid added hemline bulk.

KICK-PLEATED SKIRT

Be inventive and knit a skirt with kick pleats—two in front and two in back. The skirt should fit smoothly over the hipline; so compute your measurements carefully. It does not adapt well to bulky yarns or complicated pattern stitches.

96. Two-seam skirt with slip-stitch gores.

97. Three-piece ensemble. Knitted of red-charcoal tweed wool yarn, with red pleat inserts. V-neck cardigan, classic turtleneck pullover, kick-pleated skirt. Red slip-stitch crochet trim on cardigan and pleat inserts. Designed and knitted by author. Photo by Larry Rea.

Divide the total waist measurement by 4 and add 2 stitches for the seam allowance. Vertical rows of slip stitches form the turnback for the pleat. The kick pleat is formed in sections and is sewn in, rather than knitted in. Here's how.

Cast on the appropriate number of stitches for one panel. With right side facing you, knit 1 stitch, slip the next stitch as if to purl, knit across to the last 2 stitches, slip the next stitch as if to purl, and knit the last stitch. On the right side of your knitting, always begin with knit 1, slip 1 and end with slip 1, knit 1.

Begin increasing about 2 inches down from the waistline. Increase 1 stitch *after* the first slip 1, and *before* the last slip 1. Work to a point 4 or 5 inches above the knee. Determine how wide you want the pleat. For a 2-inch-wide pleat, if your gauge is 6 stitches to the inch, cast on 6 stitches at the beginning of the next 2 rows. Your knitting should look like fig. 99. Continue the increases, spacing them 1½ or 2 inches apart, to the desired length before hemming. Again, knit a turning row, change to one size smaller needles, and knit the hem. Bind off loosely. Knit four identical panels.

To make 2-inch pleat inserts with a 6-stitches-to-the-inch gauge, cast on 14 stitches and knit even until the inserts are the same length as the extensions on the skirt panels (include a turning row and hem). Bind off. Make four inserts.

To assemble all the sections, pin each panel to another (right sides together) at the seam allowance and backstitch with matching yarn. Pin and stitch the pleat inserts to the extensions. Turn hem to wrong side and slip-stitch. Fold the extensions in at the vertical slip stitch and baste with contrasting yarn from waist to hem. Turn skirt to wrong side and stitch across extensions and inserts at pleat breaks. Turn skirt to right side. Top-stitch to top of pleat on each side through the vertical slip stitch. Baste pleats down and lightly steam.

To make the waistband casing, with one size smaller circular needle, pick up stitches all around the top of the assembled skirt and knit even for 2 inches. Bind off and slip-stitch loosely, leaving a 1-inch opening to insert the elastic.

The design of this skirt enables you to turn it around back

Back   Front

98. Front and back views of kick-pleated skirt.

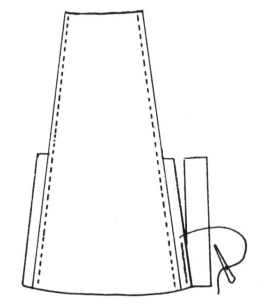

99. Attaching pleat insert.

to front and side to side, because the panels are evenly divided. To store, don't fold it—slip the waistband through the rod on a suit hanger.

DIRNDL SKIRT

Dirndl skirts go in and out of fashion, but they're comfortable and easy to knit, so let's not ignore them. They need little or no shaping—just a bit at the waist and hip, and from then on it's straight down. Dirndls are very practical for children, but they aren't for everyone. If you are short and slender or tall and slender, you can get away with the extra fullness at the waist. If you are a bit heavy around the middle, stay away from this design.

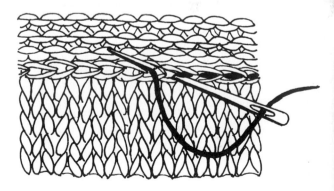

100. Top-stitching kick pleat.

67

Front   *Back*

101. Dirndl skirt.

102. Detail—zipper.

All the fullness in the dirndl occurs at the waistline and reflects at the hip line. Therefore, it is reasonable to choose a lighter-weight yarn for this design.

Measure around the widest part of the hip and divide the measurement in half. Knit a sample for gauge. For the front, cast on the number of stitches required for the hip measurement plus 2 for a seam allowance. With one size smaller needles than the gauge, knit 2 inches even for the waistband, ending on right side. Because the waistband will be folded over to the right side of the skirt, turn your work to the wrong side to start the main part of the skirt. For example: using stockinette stitch, end waistband section on the knit row. Knit the next row and continue regular stockinette stitch. Change to gauge needles, and work even to the desired length. Knit a turning row, change back to the smaller needles, and knit the hem. Knit the back in two sections (see A-line skirt), and cast on 2 seam-allowance stitches for *each* back panel. Work same as front. Sew the seams; turn hem to wrong side and slip-stitch. Turn the waistband casing to right side, fold in half, and neatly overcast in place, leaving a small opening at one of the side seams or at the center front for inserting a drawstring. To make a drawstring, crochet or braid several strands of yarn together. Knot each end and weave one end through the casing.

ZIPPER INSERTION

You may choose to insert a zipper in the side or middle back seam of your knitted skirt, so you should know how to do it. Remember, you won't be able to turn the skirt around if it has a zipper.

For either a back or side opening, start sewing the seam about 6½ inches below the waistband. (Sew the other seams after inserting the zipper.) After the appropriate seam is sewn, single crochet once around the opening, pulling in any loose knitted stitches as you go. To make a lap placket, crochet another row on the left side facing you. Fasten off. Turn the two sewn sections to the wrong side and lightly steam the seam, flattening it with your fingers. Let it dry thoroughly; then pin the zipper to the placket. If it will make you feel more secure, first pin the zipper, and then baste it down. With matching yarn or thread, backstitch the zipper into the opening. Tack the bottom of the lap in place. Sew the remaining seams, hem, and then block as usual

Let me remind you to be alert to the fiber content of your yarn. If you plan to knit with pure wool, you have some breathing space to stretch or shrink the sizing, if necessary, with steam. For cotton, linen, synthetics, or combinations of any of these, you must knit to fit, because these fibers *cannot* be manipulated.

To add some sizzle to your skirt designs, innovate. Dramatize a plain gored skirt by including a cable stitch at

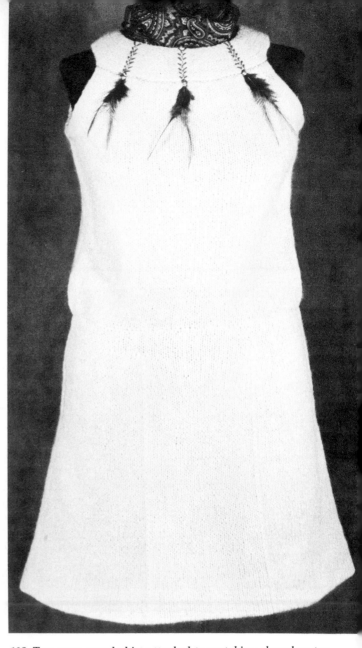

103. Two-seam gored skirt attached to matching sleeveless top. Neckline stitchery detail designed by Beverly Rush. Garment recycled and designed by author. Photo by Beverly Rush.

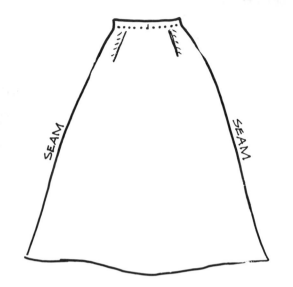

104. Darts outside of marker.

105. Darts inside of marker.

regular intervals. However, keep this in mind—a cable will automatically draw the material in; so you must compensate by adding extra stitches to your original calculations. Knit a sample to see how much your gauge might change. Or make each panel in alternating colors. Or knit horizontal stripes and carry out the theme in a sweater or jacket.

Each of the skirts described in this chapter may be attached to a knitted top without spoiling the original design. Also, each is a classic and won't go out of style before you've finished knitting it.

Alterations are relatively easy because they are knitted from the waist down, rather than from the bottom up. Should you want to shorten your skirt, with contrasting yarn, run a basting stitch around the desired length, remove the hem and seam stitching, rip back to the basting, pick up all the stitches, and knit a new hem. Wind the excess yarn in a ball and save it for another time.

To lengthen, instead of taking the whole skirt apart, just remove the slip stitching from the hem, remove the seam stitching for a few inches, rip out the bound-off row, hem, and turning row (if there is one), and put the needle back through all the loops. Make sure you don't twist the stitches when you put them back on the needle. Now add as many inches as necessary plus the hem. Restitch the seams, turn back and stitch the hem, give it a bit of blocking, and your skirt is as good as new!

Now aren't you glad you bought that extra ball of yarn when you planned your outfit? I can't tell you how many times I've been grateful for a little foresight.

DARTS

Because knitted clothing is flexible, darts are not usually necessary; however, you should know how to make them. The easiest darts are knitted in.

The basic A-line skirt is designed for gradual fullness. To make two darts, work on the outside of two marked stitches.

Divide the number of stitches in half and place a marker at that spot. Divide the stitches again on each side of the center marker, place markers, and remove the first (middle) marker. Knit across to the stitch before the first marker; pick up the bottom loop from that next stitch (the loop is actually the stitch made on the preceding row). Knit in the back of the picked-up loop, then knit in the back of the loop on the needle. Slip the marker from the left-hand needle to the right-hand needle.

Knit across the row to the other marker; slide the marker to the right-hand needle and repeat the process. You have increased 1 stitch on the outside of each marker on 1 row. Work these increases every fourth row until the darts are the desired length—4 or 5 inches, or to the top of the hipbone.

For a dart on the inside of each marker, work across to the first marker, slide the marker to the right-hand needle, increase as described above, work across to the stitch before the second marker, increase, slide the marker, and complete the row.

For a more rapidly expanding dart (useful for heavier hips and thighs), increase on each side of each marker. You'll be adding 4 stitches instead of 2. For greater expansion work these increases every other row instead of every fourth row.

If you know your stitch gauge it's easy to compute the amount of extra width you'll need. For instance, with a 6-stitches-to-an-inch gauge, by adding 2 stitches per row you've increased the width by $1/_3$ inch. This should give you an idea of how darts work.

After you've completed the darts, hold the material up against you and flatten the edges near your hipbone. Does the material feel and look wide enough? If not, you're better off ripping and starting over with more stitches.

Should you decide to knit the skirt starting at the hem and working up, simply decrease at the markers, rather than increase. Plan the darts to begin near the upper hipbone. The effect is the same. Add the waistband by picking up stitches with a smaller needle after working all the pieces.

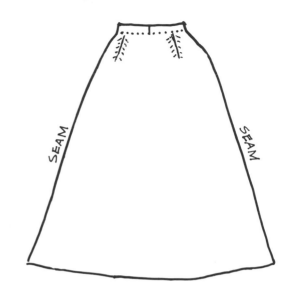

106. Darts on both sides of marker.

Squared-off Wearables

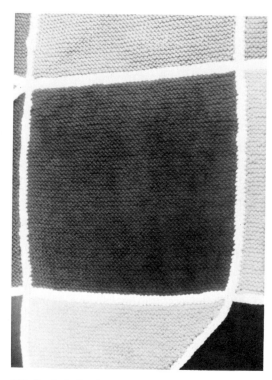

107. Basic knitted square.

Knitted squares can be put together in many ways for a completely original garment that is elegant, practical, and, better still, timeless. By assembling squares of the same or different colors and textures, you can make whole wardrobes of handsome knits—ponchos, caftans, skirts, sweaters, jackets, coats, and tunics—for men, women, and children. And squared-off knitting frees you to alter hemlines, sleeves, and widths just by adding or subtracting squares. See fig. C4.

For your first squared-off knitting project, use a flat yarn, such as wool knitting worsted, and knit all the squares in garter stitch. Knit some samples, as usual, to determine your stitch gauge. For a 12-inch square, with a stitch gauge of 6 stitches to the inch on a number 6 or 7 needle, cast on 60 stitches. Work forth and back until the piece measures 12 inches vertically. Bind off.

Here's how to measure to decide how many squares you'll need for a basic dress. From the collarbone, run the tape measure down the body to the desired finished length. Measure across the chest loosely—underarm to underarm.

We'll assume the vertical measurement is 48 inches and the chest measurement is 22 inches. Eight 12-inch squares should be ample for the front of the garment; use 8 more for the back plus 4 for both sleeves. The wool yarn will relax a bit when it is blocked; so you will have enough fabric for a small seam allowance. For longer sleeves, knit 4 more

108. Half-knitted square made into triangle.

squares—2 for each sleeve, or add only half-squares. Adjust the hem the same way: add or subtract squares.

For a looser stitch, use a larger needle and cast on fewer stitches, remembering to measure your gauge to determine the number needed. Each time you switch to one size larger or smaller needles, your square, with the same number of stitches, will expand or diminish about two inches. You may want to use larger or smaller squares for your garment.

Combine squares of garter stitch with stockinette stitch for a high-low texture, or use squares of different pattern stitches together. (Be sure to gauge the pattern stitches so the squares will line up with each other.) You might even insert a pattern block in the center of a plain square.

Lightweight garments of cotton, linen, or synthetics, knitted using the squared-off method, can be very exciting. Knit the squares with a medium- or lightweight yarn on a larger needle, and you'll have a lacy fabric that is ideal for warmer weather. These yarns have little or no resilience; so do consider that when planning the size of the squares. Don't try to stretch them to fit—you will only distort the material.

SQUARE MAGIC

Here's a formula for knitting magic squares. With this formula, it isn't necessary to count rows because the square

109. Magic square.

110. *Magic-square shawl. Knitted of odds and ends of mohair in orange, beige, hot pink, green, and black. Designed and knitted by Mary Dean Scott.*

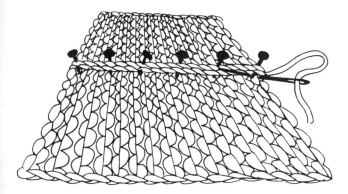

111. *Backstitching squares.*

is formed automatically. With an even number of stitches, cast on twice the number you will need for the size square you wish. For a 10-inch square, using knitting worsted and a number 8 needle with a gauge of 5 stitches to the inch, cast on 100 stitches. Place a marker at 50 stitches. For row 1, knit to within 2 stitches of marker, knit the next 2 stitches together, slip marker to right-hand needle, k next 2 stitches together, and complete row. Knit row 2. Continue working these 2 rows, decreasing 1 stitch each side of the marker as described in row 1, until all the stitches are used up. Fasten off the last stitch. Like magic, your square will be formed (fig. 109).

Make magic squares with more than one color by tying in another color whenever and wherever you choose. Make a two-color square by knitting it half-and-half. Or knit half the square with flat yarn and the other half with textured yarn. There are infinite ways to combine color and texture; so play around with some of these possibilities. I guarantee the surprising results will delight you.

Notice that the double decreases form an openwork diagonal line. When you are ready to assemble the squares, sew them together with all the diagonals in the same direction, or alternate them. With magic squares, you can add pattern and color variations with very little effort.

Reliable garter stitch is best for this technique because the edges remain flat, making the assembling process easier. However, you should give stockinette stitch a try. Although the edges will curl, careful assembling will take care of them, and you'll have a nice contrast.

You have many assembling choices, and so you can

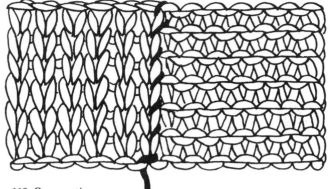

112. Overcasting squares.

achieve various effects. Crochet together squares of different colors, using a master color for the joining yarn. Or backstitch them together so there is a right and wrong side to your knitted fabric.

Make all the squares in one color for a monochromatic effect; then add textural interest by assembling them with the knitting going in opposite directions. Sew them together with a deeper or lighter shade of the original color.

Are the color combinations hard to visualize? Lay out all the pieces on a flat surface and move them around like checkers until the composition pleases you. Be daring with your arrangement.

Don't try to block the squares before you put them together. It's too risky, especially if you are a novice. For better control, connect all the pieces, matching up the edges, and then block the finished garment.

When you've knitted the correct number of squares, pin those for the front together and sew. Next do the same for the back. Connect the back to the front at the shoulders, leaving about 8 inches at the center for the neck opening. If you plan to insert a zipper for either a back or front opening, leave a 6- or 7-inch opening at the center seam. The zipper should be sewn in after blocking.

Sew or crochet the underarms and two side seams, and add a crocheted edge if you like. And that's all there is to it!

To turn the dress into a tunic, leave the side seams open 8 or 10 inches above the hem.

Squared-off knitting is practical for constructing a coat or jacket. Leave the center front seam open, and finish off the

75

113. Magic-square shawl knitted of mohair in electric blue, periwinkle, orange, and gold. Decorated with fringe (see fig. 114). Designed and knitted by Mary Dean Scott.

114. Back view of shawl in fig. 113.

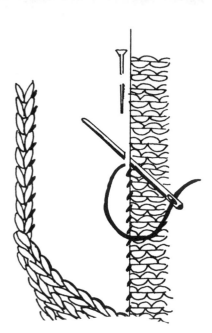

115. Sewing grosgrain ribbon facing.

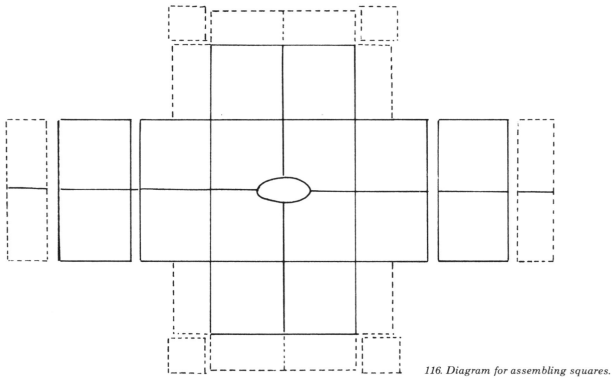

116. Diagram for assembling squares.

front-opening edges with single crochet. After the garment is blocked, tack a strip of grosgrain ribbon along the wrong side of each edge to prevent curling.

Want pockets? Knit more squares, either the same size as those in the body or smaller, and sew them on wherever you please. Use matching yarn to conceal the stitches. Or crochet an edge and then sew the pocket on.

How about a belt? Cast on 12 or 14 stitches and knit back and forth for 50 inches (or any length you prefer). Belts get lots of wear so use a smaller needle for firmer texture.

Squared-off knitting is easy to adjust, and you can change the look of the garment by simply rearranging squares or by adding or subtracting them.

Use up leftover yarns from other projects with this technique, and don't worry about color arrangement. Watch for yarn sales. You can often pick up great bargains. Yarn shops frequently have close-out baskets of discontinued yarns that you can pick up for a fraction of their original cost—and you don't have to worry about matching dye lots.

Don't Throw It Away!

What could be more creative than making something new from something old. At least half of my hand knits have been other designs in a previous life, and I never throw anything away. Fig. 128 was originally a basic long-sleeved turtleneck sweater which had been buried in a drawer for years. I couldn't stand the thought of all that yarn going to waste; so one day I ripped out the whole thing, washed the yarn, and reknitted it into a contemporary design.

Update an out-of-style jacket of woven material by removing the sleeves and knitting new ones in a matching or contrasting yarn. Use the woven sleeves as a guide for the knitted sleeves. The new sleeves won't look like orphans if you trim the neckline or collar (if there is one) with a matching knitted binding. Or knit new pockets and stitch them to the jacket.

Does the jacket have a companion skirt that doesn't fit? Work some more magic by inserting knitted gussets along the side seams, or stitch a knitted strip down the center of the skirt.

Add a woven sleeve to a outdated sweater. First, carefully remove the stitching from the sleeve seams, and, using the old sleeves as guides, cut sleeves from your new material. Insert the new sleeve into the armhole, and hand or machine stitch it to the sleeve opening. Add some decorative embroidery to conceal the join. Use the same embroidery theme elsewhere on the garment as a complementary feature.

Nothing has to go to waste. The scraps left over from your remodeling projects may be converted into many useful articles: toss pillows, place mats, throws for the sofa, knitted caps or belts, and even knitted or crocheted soft jewelry. Decorate edges with tassels or fringes.

UNRAVELING

A true bonus of hand knitting is the ease with which it may be converted from old to new by unraveling the yarn and knitting it over again. There's a sense of adventure in using previously knitted yarns to create a completely different design or, with a bit of imagination, updating an old sweater or skirt.

Unraveling yarns can also be a therapeutic venture. It requires minimum concentration but allows you time to daydream or to mentally design your next project.

When I am in a hurry, and the creative juices are flowing, instead of making a trip to the yarn shop I rummage around in my closet for a neglected hand knit, unravel it, and knit something completely different. The skirt in fig. C14 was originally knit many years ago. Since then it has been reknitted three times, each time in a different shape. Fig. 122 shows the original design.

Many of you probably have just such a treasure tucked away—one that you couldn't bear to part with because it

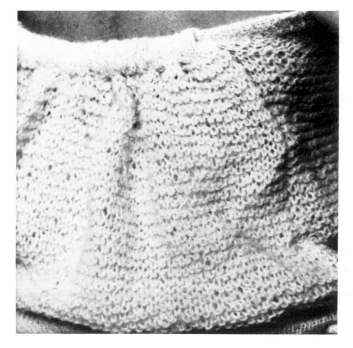

117. Back view of halter top. See front in fig. C13.

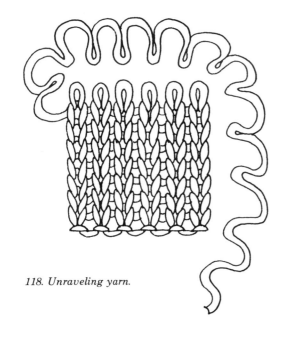

118. Unraveling yarn.

119. Hank of yarn after washing.

was a favorite. But it's limp and tired and shopworn so you've relegated it to the bottom of a drawer. For heaven's sake, get it out, rip it up, wash the yarn, and use it over again.

It takes time to pull out all the seams and undo the knitted fabric, but be assured the results are worthwhile—and you'll have the fun and challenge of inventing something entirely new!

My friend Mary Scott scrounges thriftshops for discarded hand knits or odd balls of yarn. The exquisite shawls in figs. 110, 113, and 114 illustrate her imaginative use of leftovers.

Most hand-knitted sweaters are knitted from the bottom hem to the shoulder, and the sleeves from cuff to shoulder. Exceptions are sweaters knitted on circular needles, from the neckline down, without side seams. So before you start to unravel, check to see how the sweater was knitted. Hold the material firmly on either side of one seam. Start from the bottom and remove all the seam stitching, tugging the material in opposite directions so the stitching is more visible. Cut only the anchor stitch, or undo it if you can find the end. Make sure you don't cut the fabric. With your tapestry needle or the point of a skinny knitting needle, work the sewing yarn out of the seam. Release all connecting seams this way. After all the pieces are separated, find the bound-off edge of one shoulder and undo the last stitch; then start unraveling. As you unravel, wind the yarn around a large book or around the back of a chair. Tie it in three or four places and slide it off the book or chair. It will be crimped from previous knitting, but don't be upset. Careful launder-

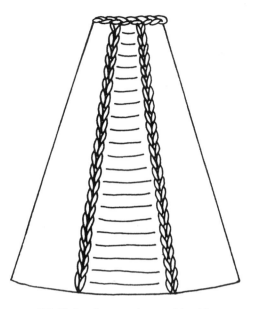

120. *Knitted gusset inserted in skirt.*

ing will usually remove the dents. Don't wind the hanks too thickly, because the drying time will be just that much longer.

Next, wash the yarn. Fill a basin with lukewarm water to which has been added a capful of mild liquid soap—*no detergent!* Swish the yarn around in the suds for a minute or two; then gently squeeze out the excess water. Rinse in cool water, changing the water several times until the final rinse is clear.

Again, squeeze out the excess water—never wring—and roll the yarn in a large, thirsty bath towel. Leave the washed yarn wrapped in the towel for 15 or 20 minutes to absorb even more water; then hang the yarn over plastic or padded hangers. I hang my recycled yarn over the bathtub and let any remaining moisture drip into the tub. If you have a laundry tub, that's even better. Don't hang it outdoors. The drying process may take a day or two, but for goodness' sake, don't try to speed things up by putting the yarn in the dryer. Instant disaster. You'll have felt instead of knitting yarn.

Every few hours, turn the yarn to allow the air to circulate, and when it is completely dry, wind it loosely into a ball. Now you're all ready to start your new project.

A note about synthetic yarn. Sometimes washing doesn't remove the crimps; so you have a choice. Use it "as is" and create a surprise texture, or slide the yarn over the end of your ironing board and lightly steam it by holding the iron a couple of inches above the yarn and smoothing the yarn with your fingers. Never put the hot iron directly on the

121. *Crocheted gusset in sweater body.*

122. *"Before" view of suit in of fig. C14. Photo by Larry Rea*

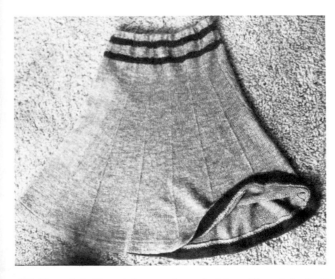

123. *Recycled skirt with cut-and-stitched hem. See original skirt in fig. 122.*

yarn—especially a synthetic, because the synthetic fibers could melt. You'd really have a mess and would probably ruin the surface of your iron, too.

By the way, if you don't have a convenient tub, use two cake racks hooked together or your broiler rack, with a towel underneath, as a drying surface.

STITCH-AND-CUT

You may not want to take time to unravel a pullover sweater that has seen better days, but you can convert it to a wearable cardigan.

Lay the sweater on a flat surface, and find the exact center front from neckline to hem. Trace the center stitch with a basting thread all the way down the front. With your sewing machine set on the longest stitch, sew 2 double rows of stitching close together and parallel to each other on each side of the basting line. Carefully cut along the basting. The double rows of stitching prevent the fabric from raveling.

Now you are ready to finish the raw edges. Fold each cut edge to the wrong side and stitch. Add a row of single crochet along each center edge to form a firm base for the new border. Be sure to use yarn with the same fiber content. Pick up stitches along each edge and knit facings (including buttonholes), or insert a zipper. Add some colorful buttons and you've given that old sweater a whole new life.

Use the stitch-and-cut technique to add a gusset to a skirt or to make a sweater larger with gusset inserts at the side seams. Conceal the joins with some decorative embroidery.

Replace worn-out sleeves by the same method. Stitch

double rows around the armholes; then cut off the old sleeves. Turn the raw edges under as previously described; then knit new sleeves and stitch them to the armhole.

KNITTING FABRIC STRIPS

Knitting with woven material is a crackerjack way to use up remnants of previous sewing projects.

Lay your material out on a flat surface and cut ½-inch strips from the bias. Glue one strip onto another, end to end, preferably with a liquid glue made especially for fabric. It's very strong, you need just a drop, and it dries almost instantly. Roll the glued fabric strips into a ball. Or take the lazy way out, use no glue, and join them as you work the same way you would join in a new ball of yarn. Weave in all the loose ends later on.

Try fabric knitting with different sizes of needles just to see what happens. Then try some of the pattern stitches. The look of a printed fabric will change considerably as you change needle sizes. Fig. 126 is an old purple and white sheet cut on the bias and worked in stockinette stitch on number 10 needles. Record your findings in your notebook.

Metal needles are easier to use with fabric than plastic needles. The points are more defined, and the stitches seem to glide more smoothly over the metal. Using plastic needles with synthetic materials can cause friction, which, in turn, makes the material stick to the needles.

My experiments in knitting wool woven fabric produced an unexpected result. I found out quickly that very narrow strips were not successful, because the constant tugging of

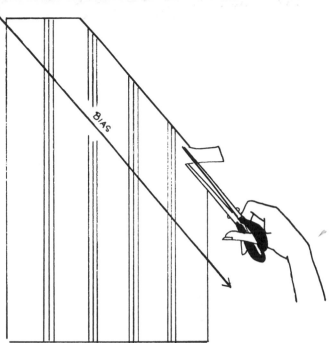

124. Cutting bias fabric strips.

125. Gluing fabric strips.

126. Knitted fabric strips.

the material caused the material to separate and break. So cut your strips wider (about ¾ inch) and use larger needles (size 13 or larger), depending on the type and texture of the wool. Be gentle.

Heavy woolens, such as coat fabrics, and thick-and-thins are clumsy to work with and are not easily manipulated, but try them anyway, just to satisfy your own curiosity.

There's no perfect method for computing the amount of woven material you'll need. But for a ball-park figure, measure off a specific amount of material, cut all the strips, glue them together (or not), and knit up that amount. Then measure the length and width of your sample and estimate from that. Or take a chance and use whatever you have. The finished product could be an interestingly original combination of pattern and texture.

Make certain to combine like materials to avoid laundering problems. Wash and dry new cotton material before cutting strips to avoid shrinkage later on. New wool should be steamed.

Knitted woven fabric has more density than knitted yarn; so rather than struggling to sew the seams with your tapestry needle, connect the seams with a threaded sharp needle designed for sewing leather and suede. You can try zigzagging the seams on the sewing machine, or you can crochet them together.

Knit squares of fabric strips, and assemble them into a tunic or overblouse (see "Squared-off Wearables"). Use them to design children's garments. They make wonderful pillows and bed throws.

Once you learn to handle knitted woven strips comfortably, ideas will come more readily, and your remnants will soon disappear.

ODDS AND ENDS

Use beads or sequins to turn a blah sweater into a fashionable evening sweater. First work a simple outlining embroidery stitch in circles all over the body of the garment; then sew beads or sequins to the center of the circles. Packets of beads and sequins are available at most yarn shops or sewing centers.

Turn a striped sweater into a plaid by running a crocheted slip stitch vertically through the knit fabric at spaced intervals. Or with a threaded tapestry needle, weave yarn vertically through the fabric. Use one or more colors to define the plaid.

Add a ribbing to a woven blouse or jacket. Pick up stitches along the edge of the woven material and knit down, or knit the ribbing separately and sew it on (fig. 127).

Turn an old sweater into an instant blouson. If the sweater has a ribbing at the bottom, stitch-and-cut (page 82) the ribbing away from the garment, fold back the cut edge about 1 inch, and tack to wrong side, leaving a small opening in the front or on one side. Slide a drawstring through the casing, knot the ends, and that's all there is to it (fig. 128)!

127. Handwoven blouson. Hand-knitted cuffs and waistband. Designed by Deborah Ann Abbott for Aurora Designs. Photo by Packard Studio.

128. Blouson—a recycled classic turtleneck pullover. Camel sport-weight wool. Alternating squares of knit and purl. Crocheted drawstring. Designed and knitted by author.

85

Make your own drawstring by crocheting a cord from the garment yarn. Or knit a three-stitch cord. Cast 3 stitches onto a medium-sized, double-pointed needle. Knit across the 3 stitches and, instead of turning your work, slide the stitches to the opposite end of the needle and knit them again. Work this way until the cord is long enough for your sweater. Bind off, and weave the loose ends back into the cord. Knot the ends (fig. C3).

Spool-knit a cord, using an old sewing-thread spool. Pound 4 nails into one end of the spool. Drop the cut end of the yarn through the hole, and wrap the yarn around each nail once. Working from right to left, lay the working yarn above the loop on the first nail. With a crochet hook, lift the bottom loop up and over the working yarn and the nail. Work this way, round and round, until your cord is the desired length. Cut the yarn and weave the cut end through the loops on the nails; then lift the loops off the nails, and knot the end. To make a fatter cord, add more nails to the spool.

Reversibles are big news, and so warm and practical when it's nippy outside. Turn a jacket into a reversible by lining it with an old cardigan. First remove the woven lining from the jacket (if there is one); then, with the wrong side of the sweater facing the wrong side of the jacket, overcast all the edges of the sweater to the jacket. If the sweater sleeves are long enough, expose the cuffs below the edge of the jacket sleeve, and stitch the sleeve to the jacket sleeve just above the ribbing. Cover any worn spots with decorative embroidery, and the jacket/sweater will look brand-new.

Do you live in an area where the winters are long and severe? Make some fashionable boot cuffs from your leftover wool yarns. Measure the circumference at the top of the calf; then knit a sample to determine your stitch gauge, and cast on the correct number of stitches, less 1 inch. For example, if the measurement is 13 inches and your gauge is 5 stitches to the inch, cast on 60 stitches. Work even, in single or double ribbing, for about 18 inches. Bind off. Sew the two long side edges together with matching yarn, fold the cuffs over 4 or 5 inches, and there you are. Stay warm!

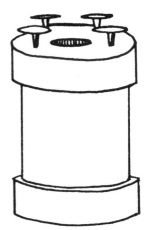

129. Knitting spool.

130. Knitting spool with cord in progress.

Use the sleeves from an old sweater to make boot cuffs if you don't feel like knitting them. Remove the sleeves from the body of the sweater by undoing the armhole seams. Then stitch-and-cut (page 82) across the sleeve material, where the armholes start and also just above the sweater cuffs. Turn raw edges to the wrong side and slip-stitch with compatible yarn. Fold the top of the sleeves over: instant boot cuffs!

Now you have the remainder of the sweater to transform into a warm headband. Remove the side seams, and measure off a section about 5 inches wide and long enough to fit around your head. Stitch-and-cut around this area. Fold the piece in half lengthwise with the wrong side out, and stitch the short edges together.

If the ribbing of the sweater hasn't lost too much elasticity, stitch-and-cut it away from the sweater. Add a crocheted edge to neaten it up, stitch the short edges together, and there's your headband.

Do you still have some leftover sweater parts? Don't toss them out, stitch-and-cut squares, diamonds, or rectangles, and use them to patch other sweaters or as knitted pockets for woven garments.

Have these few ideas set you to thinking of other ways to recycle your knits? Go to it.

132. Spool-knit cord used for lacing.

133. Boot cuffs made from double strands of white mohair.

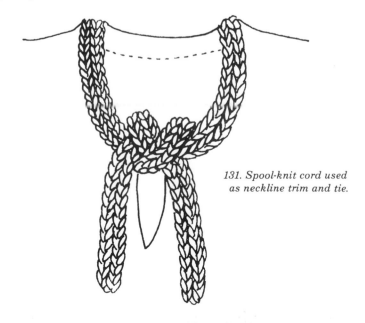

131. Spool-knit cord used as neckline trim and tie.

Taking Care of Your Knits

Proper care and storage of your valuable hand knits is essential if they are to retain their shape and texture.

Before laundering or dry cleaning, be sure to read the yarn labels. I urge you to attach labels to all the garments you make. List the fiber content and cleaning instructions.

I prefer to wash my hand knits, because frequently, and sometimes disastrously, dry-cleaning solvents leave a film and a not-too-pleasant odor on the fibers.

Before laundering, draw an outline of the garment on a sheet of white paper, and lay the paper outline on top of a large bath towel. You'll come back to it later.

When laundering any knit, handle it as little as possible, because the weight of the water can completely distort the original shape. Turn the garment inside out before washing; then squeeze it gently in the suds. Always use a mild, pure liquid soap in cool or lukewarm water. Rinse carefully two or three times until the final rinse water is clear. Squeeze out the excess moisture—never wring. Roll the garment in a large towel and let it rest for a few minutes.

Put the laundered knit on the paper outline, moving it with your fingers to conform to the outline.

When the garment is partially dry, turn it over so that the air can reach the other side. If the paper is too soggy, draw another outline on a clean sheet and throw away the old one. You may have to turn the garment two or three times before it is thoroughly dry. To hasten this process, I've sometimes resorted to the help of my hair dryer, *turned to the lowest heat*. Hold the dryer a couple of inches above the material and rotate it over the whole area. (Don't put the dryer directly on the material!) Do this for just a few minutes on each side; then let it dry naturally. If all this extra care seems like a lot of trouble, it is—but it's worth it.

Some of the new wools are now machine-washable and dryable. Follow the instructions on the yarn label exactly, and when the dryer stops, immediately remove the garment and let it rest awhile on a flat surface before storing it.

Before putting your hand knits in a drawer or closet, fold them carefully and tuck tissue paper between the folds to avoid unsightly creases. It's unwise to store knits in plastic bags, because a sealed bag traps moisture that could harm the fibers. Protect them from dust by placing an old sheet on top of your folded garments.

My personal knit wardrobe is so extensive that adequate storage has always been a problem. When I run out of drawer or shelf space, I fold knits vertically and hang one sweater or skirt over another on padded hangers and hang them in the closet. So far, I've never had a problem with sagging and they're always fresh and ready to wear. Fig. C14 shows a 15-year-old hand knit that has been stored in this manner ever since it was originally made.

Knits need to breathe, so if you can, hang them outdoors every once in a while. On a nice day, drape a clean sheet over the clothesline, then fold the garments over the sheet. Leave them for a half-hour or so; then fold them carefully and put them back in the drawer or closet

Frequent wear often causes knits to pill. When this happens, pick the nubs off by hand. Or better yet, shave them off with an electric razor, working it over the material with a circular movement. The razor will not damage the yarn. The first time I tried the electric-shaver treatment, I forgot to clean the razor afterward. My husband had a real surprise the next time he tried to use it. After that, I acquired one of my own. If you don't have an electric shaver, try a wire dog-grooming brush. They're pretty harsh; so brush gently so as not to damage the fibers.

134. Using electric razor to remove pilling.

A Note on Knitting—and Weaving and Stitchery

Jean Wilson, Beverly Rush, and I have been friends for a long time, and it was our common interest in fibers that first brought us together. Jean is a weaver, Bev a stitchery artist.

As we became close friends, we discovered that our attitudes toward our individual crafts were remarkably compatible. We decided to pool our efforts and resources in order to write the first books of the Connecting Threads series, *Knit with Style, Stitch with Style,* and *Weave with Style.* While we were working on the books we created an ensemble to demonstrate how the connecting threads of weaving, stitchery, and knitting all fit together.

Jean and I designed the long knitted jacket and handwoven skirt, and Bev designed the surface embroidery. The ensemble was created for Jean and, because Jean becomes attached to her clothes, we agreed that the outfit would be a classic that will be wearable for a long time. We selected a beautiful charcoal wool for the jacket and combined it with a companion shade of the same yarn for the skirt material. Jane Thompson did the knitting, Barbara Doyon the weaving. After the outfit was completed, Bev added the embroidery.

Working with these two marvelous artists has been an invigorating experience for me. We seem to complement one another, and I hope that our joy and success in combining crafts and skills will stimulate others to do the same. I predict you'll find some ideas in this book that will not only encourage you to knit beautiful clothing but will encourage you to think about combining knitting with other fiber crafts.

I have brought you some of my personal feelings about the wonderfully satisfying craft of knitting to expose you to avenues of design you may not have explored, and to release you from any inhibitions you might harbor about your own capabilities. Creative possiblities are nearly infinite—there are few limitations. So pick up your knitting needles and *Knit with Style*!

135. Knitted jacket with handwoven sleeves, stitchery embellishment. Designed by Jean Wilson, Beverly Rush, Ferne Cone. Knitting by Jane Thompson, stitchery by Beverly Rush, weaving by Barbara Doyon.